IMPROV COMEDY

BY ANDY GOLDBERG

FOREWORD BY JOHN RITTER

SAMUEL FRENCH ✦ HOLLYWOOD
New York ✦ London ✦ Toronto

First Edition

Library of Congress Cataloging-in-Publication Data

Goldberg, Andy, 1950-
Improv comedy / by Andy Goldberg
p.   cm.
1. Improvisation (Acting) 2. Stand-up comedy. I. Title.
PN2071.I5G65   1992   792'.028—dc20   91-41442

ISBN: 0-573-60608-0

Cover design by Heidi Frieder

Printed and bound in the United States of America

10 9 8 7 6 5

Published and distributed by
Samuel French Trade
7623 Sunset Blvd.
Hollywood, CA 90046

For My Parents

CONTENTS

FOREWORD

IMPROV

I is for Imagination, which we can plainly see,

M is for Make Believe, which usually works for me.

P is for Play Hard for all that it is worth,

R is for Recycle 'cuz we're choking Mother Earth.

O is for Opposites, which are funnier than the sames,

V is for Viola, the mother of all theater games,
    and

E is for Excel *if* you practice what you reach.

Put it all together and that spells **IMPROV** with an **E**.

This book by Andy Goldberg lays down those fun-damn-mentals of Improv Comedy and is excellent food for thought.

So my advice to those so inclined:

1. Eat this book.
2. Chew on it.
3. Then go out and play . . .
4. *Your* way.

Listen to the laughter,

John Ritter

READ THIS FIRST

People are attracted to improvisational comedy for various reasons. The study and performance of "improv" are excellent means of sharpening acting skills and invaluable to developing writing techniques. Actors praise improvisation for its help at auditions, for making them stretch, for allowing them to find new types of roles to play, and for providing a form of acting outlet that, once mastered, requires little or no rehearsal. Improv is popular for its reward of instant gratification. To reap that reward, however, one must spend a great deal of time learning and practicing the techniques.

Writers are intrigued by the process of improvisation, a form of writing on their feet. Since they are usually behind the scenes, writers enjoy a chance to say the lines themselves, rather than being relegated to sit in the audience and listen to someone else get the laugh. Writers also find that improv stimulates them to discover new ideas. The many avenues of plot and characterization explored in a single improv session provide them with an active approach to "hear dialogue" and "see action" in any number of situations.

The improv environment is also stimulating to people in various other professions. Students of mine have learned to apply improvisational techniques to their particular line of work, whether it be acting, writing, lecturing, selling, or dealing with clients. People are interested in sharpening their wit and developing their sense of humor to make them feel more confident socially and to help them deal with coworkers and business associates in a more casual and good-spirited manner.

Finally, of course, are those who have experienced an improvisational comedy show and want to learn to participate in perhaps the most organic form of comedy theater, as well as in something that is a heck of a lot of fun.

Whether or not you intend to get involved in the theater, you'll benefit from paying more attention to what is going on around you, and more than likely you'll be amused by what you begin to see. Whatever your field, you will find improvisational comedy to be an excellent means to an end as well as a highly addictive activity in itself. You will discover that, although improvisation appears to be a very loose, free form, it is actually a rather precise process that is composed of specific elements necessary to its success.

The basic idea of improv is certainly not foreign to any of us. We all improvise on a daily basis. Our life has no script, so we have to make it up as we go along. We spontaneously create what we're going to say, what we're going to do, and how we're going to deal with a given situation. Since each one of us is improvising our own life, the main thing we have to draw on for our decisions is our personality. We make many choices in our day-to-day living, but our behavior and reactions are based on who we are. We may "act" or "fake it" or even lie occasionally. Sometimes we may behave "out of character," but, basically, everything we do and say is dictated by our personality, attitude, experience, and knowledge.

When improvising for the stage, you're required to make the same kinds of choices that you make in real life. The difference is that on stage you behave and react "in character"—your decisions about what to say and what to do are determined by "What would this character say?" and "What would this character do?" The character may contain a facet of your own personality, but since the situation you're playing may have no relevance to your own life, you must be prepared to assume a role appropriate to the scene. The character's attitude, experience, and knowledge are up to you. As in scripted acting, you live another person's life for the moment. In this case you have the added challenge of making it up as you go along.

You'll be presented a situation and you'll be required to decide how you're going to deal with it. You'll invent the plot, create the place where it occurs, determine what role you'll play, and make up appropriate dialogue and activity to fit that circumstance. For improv to be successful, it should appear to be as natural as a real-life situation. So the key to successful improv theater, it would seem, is to completely assume the role of a person so specific that what you say and do comes naturally to the character you are playing.

Just as our daily life improvisation is sometimes more creative or interesting than at other times, so is what we choose to perform on stage. In real life, we usually rise to the occasion when we're put on the spot—like when we have to come up with an excuse for why we can't give a friend a ride to the airport at 5:00 A.M., or convince a new client to let us handle his account, or cancel a date with someone we wish we hadn't agreed to go out with in the first place. Situations that provide conflict in our life cause us to be creative in our efforts to deal with them. Conflict in a situation also causes it to be "dramatic." Those types of dramatic moments make for good theater.

Improvisational comedy theater requires that a situation also be funny or at least amusing, or clever, or wacky, or satirical or parodical, or impressionistic, or biting, or poignant, or insightful, or innovative in some way connected to the situation. Funny, of course, is in the bone of the beholder, but by studying the techniques of improv comedy you can learn to discover and implement your particular sense of humor. If you can see humor in the world around you, then you can also generate it.

The heart of improvisational comedy is spontaneous creativity, so nothing in this book is meant to restrict you in any way. Use this book as a guide, but wander off by yourself sometimes to explore new territory on you own.

I have endeavored here to include all the basic concepts of improv. As I was writing, however, I came to realize that for every so called "rule" of improvisation, I could think of an example of how it might be appropriate to break that rule. Therefore, my only firm rule of improv is that you will sometimes break the rest of the rules. After all, a rule is only something that has proved to work well in the past. Before you do start breaking the rules, however, try playing by them because in most cases I think you'll find that they work. If you find something is working well, contrary to a rule, then go ahead and ignore that rule for the moment. Don't change it forever, but don't let it get in the way of your spontaneous creativity either. In a performance, your audience is your barometer. If you're enjoying what you're doing and the audience is enjoying it as well, then it's working. If, however, you're having a fine time while the audience has lost interest, or at the expense of a fellow performer, then you might want to consider moving in another direction.

Above all, a good improviser should strive to be a good actor. The same skills should be applied. If your performance isn't believable, it won't be nearly as pointed. I think you'll find that when the love of getting a laugh meets the love of the acting craft, it will be a very rewarding performing experience. Performing improv comedy is the most fun I have in public. I hope you have fun with it, too.

ACKNOWLEDGMENTS

I first learned about the process of improvisational comedy when I joined DeVera Marcus's workshop in the summer of 1975. In September of that year, she asked me to be a founding member of a group she was forming, which we named "Off The Wall." I have been performing with them ever since and have been the director of the group since 1980. We currently appear at the Melrose Improvisation in West Hollywood every Monday night. Dee also founded the group "Funny You Should Ask" in 1978, which is still enjoying a successful run at the Melrose Theater in Hollywood on Saturday nights. I have happily guested with them numerous times over the years. I have had the opportunity to learn a great deal from the very gifted members of these groups, both while sharing a stage with them and while watching them perform.

The improv structures contained in this book are a compilation of exercises and scene setups I've learned from various sources, although quite a few are based on the theater games originally created by Viola Spolin and outlined in her book *Improvisation for the Theater* (Northwestern University Press). Also included are exercises I've learned from working with members of groups from all over the country, including Off the Wall, Second City, The Committee, The Pitchel Players, The Illegitimate Theater, Funny You Should Ask, The Premise, The Groundlings, For Play,"

Nothing Sacred!, and Spaghetti Jam, as well as many I have invented myself. Teaching improv has also been a continual learning experience. The instruction of others is a lesson in itself.

My special thanks to John Ritter, a great talent, for sharing his kind words and experience in the Foreword to this tome. I am also grateful to my editor, Jim Fox, who offered a fresh eye when mine was blurred from being too close.

One cannot perform, teach, or write a book about improv comedy without being influenced by all the comedy that has come before—whether on an improv stage, film, TV, or in *Mad* magazine, I have always learned from others, even if it was what not to do. So, my thanks to everyone who has come before me, anyone who ever made me laugh, and even those who haven't, for helping me find my own laughs.

Thoughts About Improv from Some of the People I've Worked with

Improv taught me that if you keep talking long enough, you'll say something funny.
>—Jeff Franklin, Creator/Executive Producer of "Full House"

I use "yes . . .and" in my dealing with writers and producers to feed and build ideas together.
>—Paul Friedman, Associate Director, Comedy Promotion for CBS

Improv comedy was a big turning point in my writing career because it taught me to be less rigid, to free myself up, to be spontaneous, and to allow myself to take chances. As a writer, cautious is one of the worst things you can be.
>—David Issacs, Emmy-winning Writer/Producer of "Cheers," "M*A*S*H"

The great benefit of improvisation is that it not just allows you, but requires you, to take chances. The acceptance of taking such chances or risks is the first step in creativity.
>—Ken Levine, Emmy-winning Writer/Producer of "Cheers," "M*A*S*H"

I'm an actor/writer/director/comic—in other words, I'm an improviser. And I have had the joy of working with some of the best and most creative people in the world—other improvisers.

      —Dee Marcus, Founder of The Illegitimate
            Theatre, Off the Wall, Funny You
            Should Ask, and Nothing Sacred

As a producer, I often find myself having to think fast and on my feet without the opportunity of preparation. Whether dealing with a writer as we work on a script, or in hammering out a budget, I believe that the confidence I have in myself to "wing it" in varied situations is due in large part from my improv studies with Andy Goldberg.

      —Vahan Moosekian, Former actor, Producer
            of "Tour of Duty"

Like my word processor, my improvisational comedy background is an intricate part of my writing.

      —Bob Rosenfarb, Supervising Producer of
            "Who's The Boss"

My improv comedy background makes me more valuable as a director because it gives me an added edge. It helps me to bring the level of the work up another notch. By working in the moment and being in the creative process with the actors, I can embellish and bring more to the work during rehearsal while still supporting the writing. Writing itself is improv-ing in your head.

      —Judy Pioli, Producer/Writer and Director of
            "Perfect Strangers" and an original
            member of Off The Wall

Improv is a great tool for writing. That's all I can come up with on the spot.
> —Marc Sotkin, Executive Producer of "The Golden Girls" and former member of Off The Wall

In the craft of writing comedy, my experience in improvisation is of a value exceeded only by plagiarism.
> —Chris Thompson, Creator/Executive Producer of "Bosom Buddies" and an original member of Off The Wall

If you don't listen to your fellow improviser, you have nothing to respond to. You're dead meat. You're in the toilet. So when you're working with a script, you should listen to your fellow players' words as if it's the first time you're hearing them.
> —George Wendt, Star of "Cheers"

Improv is the greatest form of therapy, and is so much more fun than lying on the couch.
> —Robin Williams, Actor and former member of Off The Wall

John Ritter and Dee Marcus on ABC's late night comedy special "Completely Off The Wall." (Photo by John Livzey)

ONE

AN INTRODUCTION

Every day, we deal with all types of people doing all kinds of things: things that make us shake our heads in wonder, things that make no sense, things we are critical of, things we accept anyway. At work, at the store, driving in the car, talking on the phone, eating in restaurants, walking on the street, with our friends, with our family, or with strangers, we are confronted with remarkable situations—situations that are worth thinking about, taking a second look at—and those are just the ones we're consciously aware of. Imagine all the things going on around us while we're too absorbed in our own thoughts and problems to even notice them.

Many of the situations we are aware of are ones that we all have in common, occurrences in life that we all can relate to: simple things like brushing our teeth, driving a car, or shopping in a store. For some reason, talking about these common experiences and bringing them out into the open is funny to people. We all brush our teeth, so we are all familiar with the same things connected with the activity. Most of us floss, most of us make faces when we floss, so talking about it and doing it is funny. We can all relate to plaque. And it's a funny-sounding word. Most people drive a car, so things about driving that we all can relate to are funny—like the fact that someone who doesn't let you cut in front of him in traffic is discourteous; but if he cuts in front of you, he's a jerk. Or, when you go shopping for clothes, why is the tailor always the worst-dressed guy in the store? He comes out of some back room, his eyes trying to adjust to the light. It doesn't instill much confidence.

Life is filled with things that make us wonder, things that make us angry, things that frustrate us, things that make us laugh, things that cause us concern. All of these kinds of things are subjects for improvisational comedy. This is as true for such mundane things as brushing our teeth or driving a car as it is for such important things as civil rights or politics. In the form of a short scene, based on a premise obtained just prior to its beginning, you can spontaneously explore any situation through its characters and their attitudes. Exploring the humor in these situations on stage is improvisational comedy.

Some situations seem to stand out against the rest of everyday life. That's why most drama is about the extraordinary moments of life, the highlights, the peak moments. They are generally more interesting to watch than the everyday, methodical things we do. On the other hand, the mundane redundancies of life can be a great source for comedy. The exaggeration of a minor event will often bring out the humor in it. That is not to say that there isn't humor in big events, but a situation need not be earthshaking to make for good comedy material.

Ultimately, the subject matter is not nearly as important as how you choose to deal with it. Landing on the moon or buying a soda have equal potential when it comes to humor. By handling a mundane subject in a very serious fashion, you make it funny. You artificially inflate its importance to the point of ridicule. I will never forget the episode from "The Andy Griffith Show" in which Andy and Barney are sitting on the porch and Barney announces he's going to "go git me a bottle of pop." He spends the next five minutes discussing it—how he's "gonna git" there, how good it's gonna taste, what's he's "gonna do" when he "gits" back, does Andy want one, too? I don't even remember if he ever did go "git" the pop, but it sure was funny watching him prepare to.

Humor comes from specifics. Try to zero in on the particulars of real-life situations, whether they're big events or small ones. Try to pinpoint what is most interesting, or peculiar, or frustrating, or funny about a situation and note what types of people it involves. Sometimes the people themselves make a situation funny. Try to recognize what it is about a person that catches and holds your attention. The more you observe, the more you will be able to bring realistic behavior to your improv work. Don Knotts' character, Barney Fife, certainly made that sequence what it was. The kinds of people, places, and things that attract your attention in everyday life will also intrigue an audience when presented as characters and situations on the stage.

An improv comedy scene is the same as any other theatrical piece. It reflects some facet of life, or at least someone's perception of it. Hopefully the reflection is humorous. To present that humor on stage, and I can't make this point strongly enough: *portraying your characters and situations from a humerous point of view is more important than saying funny things.*

Sometimes you have to exaggerate an experience to make it funny, but sometimes all you have to do is tell the truth. Just report on life. The trick is in recognizing what things to report. Most funny things will call attention to themselves. Because they're odd, we take notice. A person with a peculiar-sounding voice will stand out in a crowd. Our eye automatically goes to a person with an unusual style of dress. If it weren't for their peculiarities, they would blend in with everyone else. When we walk into a situation that has something abnormal about it, we notice it right away. Start to make note of situations and people that attract your attention, for they are the stuff of which comedy is made.

THE LANGUAGE OF IMPROV

Improv comedy is presented in the form of scenes and exercises. We'll get to the exercises a little later on, but first let's talk about the "scene." The purest form of improv, the scene is a short theatrical piece comprised of character, environment, and plot that is able to stand on its own. That is to say, you can summarize any scene by describing it as someone being somewhere and doing something. That summarization is called the "premise." Every scene has a premise. A typical scene usually runs one to six minutes in length.

The "scene suggestion," "suggested premise," "audience suggestion," or "scene idea" (all names for the same thing) is the basic concept that is given prior to a scene. It may be suggested by the workshop leader, a fellow improviser, or an audience member. The suggestion may include one or more of the "elements" for the scene—such as plot, character, or environment—or may only provide a single facet of one of those elements, such as an activity or a conflict (more on this later). This information given prior to the scene is incorporated into what will become the premise of the scene.

Since the scene is then improvised, its premise may change somewhat once the scene has begun. The given information must be used in the scene, but you can now embellish the suggested premise in any way you want. For instance, the suggested premise may be "a couple celebrates their wedding anniversary." You may decide that it is their fiftieth anniversary and that they are celebrating it in a hot-air balloon. This additional information usually provides a "hook" for the scene, a wild card, a plot twist that provides a source for the comedy in the scene.

The suggested premise might be "playing Nintendo." You may choose to make the scene about parents playing the game after their kids have gone to bed. If the scene suggestion is "exploring a cave," you might play it as three Girl Scouts who are lost. The audience suggestion "watching TV" might turn out to be about a group of homeless people commenting on the programming while watching through a department-store window.

For every suggested premise, a myriad of options of how to play out the scene are possible. As long as you are faithful to the actual words of the suggestion and fulfill some interpretation of their meaning, you can do anything you like with the scene. For instance, if the scene suggestion is "first date," the most obvious interpretation may be of a boy and a girl on a first date, awkwardly getting to know each other. The scene could be teenagers at the drive-in or singles who have been fixed up having dinner at a restaurant. The couple may, however, be senior citizens—a widow and widower at a small-town dance hall—or pen pals from different countries finally meeting face to face after writing to each other for ten years. You might even take the premise in its literal sense and make the scene about a Neanderthal woman and man having The First Date.

The most improvised element of the scene, of course, is plot, for it will be constantly changing. From the above examples, though, you can see how your choices of character, environment, and activity have just as big an influence on the scene. Your only requirement is to fulfill the premise. How you do it is up to you.

Besides scenes, there are many "exercises" that can be performed. The difference between an improv exercise and a scene is that an exercise doesn't necessarily have a plot, but it usually does have some built-in structure. (The word "scene" is commonly used to describe any improv piece. So, as confusing as this may be, sometimes an exercise is also referred to as a scene.) Some exercises are not really performance-oriented enough to part be of a show, but they are very useful in the workshop when you are learning and practicing improv. An exercise is often geared toward a particular element of improv and is designed to allow the performer to concentrate on that element. A "Panel," for instance, is an example of an exercise in which several characters are being questioned about something they have in common. Because the element of plot is not relevant, and the use of the environment is limited by the fact that the people are stationary, the element of character has a chance to be explored in greater depth and becomes the source of the humor in the scene.

In some exercises, the structure involves a technique or a gimmick, which becomes the vehicle for the humor. For instance, Change of Emotions (see Workshop section, page 175) is an exercise in which the performers go through emotional transformations that are called out during a scene by the audience. The humor comes from observing how the performers change. The Hitchhiker is an exercise that literally provides a vehicle to develop a character's dialect or attitude as each performer chooses an accent or emotion for his character to use as he hitchhikes a ride. The "character" is the persona the performer takes on during a scene or an exercise. The "performer" is you. By the way, I will be using the terms "actor" and "performer" interchangeably. I will also be generally using pronouns of the male gender as a matter of convenience, not as a sexist statement.

ABOUT THIS BOOK

This first section of the book is about improv in general with some thoughts on how you can start enjoying the process. Included are some pitfalls to watch out for and some general rules of thumb. Throughout the book, I will share my experiences as a performer as well as a teacher to give examples of what has and has not worked for improvisers in the past. I'll also refer to popular movies and TV shows and their characters as examples, since they are widely known to the general public. Comedy is comedy no matter what the medium, and the same techniques apply. Just because something is improvised, its quality doesn't lessen. You should strive to make your improvised comedy meet equal standards that you would impose upon your scripted work. Use the examples of things done by other people to inspire ideas of your own. You never want to use someone else's ideas, and you never want to imitate someone else unless you make it clear that that's what you're doing. Imitation is the highest form of flattery, but "borrowing" someone else's material is the lowest form of larceny.

As you begin to improvise, you will realize what techniques work best for you and what makes you unique as an improviser. I'll explain the techniques, but the composition has to be your own. It will be a result of your own experiences and insights.

The second section of the book is for those who wish to take the plunge and perform improvisational comedy in front of an audience. It is a discussion of ways to construct an improv show with suggestions about how to assemble a capable comedy troupe. I suggest reading the performance section even if you don't intend to be in a show. It expands on ideas and techniques covered in the other sections of the book.

The third section of the book is about the workshop. It comprises exercises and scene setups, with hints on how to use them. These structures are meant for use in a show as well as in the workshop, though you will find that some adapt themselves to a performance situation more successfully than others.

The exercises and scene setups are arranged roughly in order from "beginning" to "advanced," but you should feel free to return to any as needed to reinforce technique. You may also find yourself returning to certain exercises just because you enjoy them. Most of the exercises are geared toward a group of people in a workshop environment, but elements of almost all of them can be played with a partner or even by one's self. In fact, an excellent time to practice many of the exercises—like doing voices, accents, pantomime, and discovering characters—is while you're alone, driving a car, taking a shower, or standing in front of a mirror. The Workshop section also contains simple mental exercises to get you thinking spontaneously and to help you find your sense of humor. Whether you are performing a show, studying in a traditional classroom situation, or with friends gathered in somebody's rec room, the same practices apply.

If you are not already familiar with improv exercises, take some time now to look through the Workshop section, just to get an idea of the kinds of things I'm talking about.

WEATHERING THE ELEMENTS

Some people think improv is a little like magic. They see something created from nothing, right before their eyes, so they think it's a trick. A typical comment from someone who has seen an improv show for the first time: "How did you do that? It must have been worked out before . . ."

The only thing worked out before is the process. Whereas a magician practices an illusion over and over until it is no longer visible, an improviser practices the process until it is no longer apparent. A magician spends hours off stage practicing stashing a rabbit or palming a lit cigarette. As an improviser, you create characters and practice reaction and various thought processes. The only "trick" to improv is that there is a method to the madness. Something is created from nothing, but the process to make it happen has to be learned and practiced by the performers. The more improv you do, the more proficient you become with the process until it eventually becomes second nature. When you no longer have to think about the process, you can put all your energy into the result.

An improvisational comedy scene is structured in essentially the same fashion as any written comedic or dramatic scene from a play or film or television show. It comprises the three basic elements: character, environment, and plot. These elements are dependent on sub-elements that help to flesh out the scene—things like activity, attitude, conflict, specifics, point of view, and dialogue (each of which is covered in its respective place later in the text).

In any particular scene, all three of the basic elements should be explored, since each is dependent upon the other. An improvised piece, however, is traditionally rather short and is meant to stand on its own, so there is often not time to develop all the elements to the extent that one might in an entire play. Frequently, one or two of the elements become the main thrust of the scene while the others are used to support its exploration. All scenes must establish an environment or setting. All scenes will have characters interacting in that environment, and all scenes must have a plot. But one or two of the elements may take the primary focus.

Take for example the premise "at the laundromat." The environment is a given in this particular situation, but it might not necessarily be the primary focus of the scene. You can do a hundred different scenes in a laundromat and each one would be different. Each one would have a different approach and the focus would vary. It could be closing time before your load is dry. There could be a mix up over clothes. The added plot twist that it is closing time might bring the focus of the scene onto the characters—the laundromat manager and patron may be in conflict over whether to remain open late or go home with wet socks.

In forthcoming chapters I will break down character, environment, and plot into individual elements. Each has its own influence on a scene, and each has its own developmental techniques. But, as you will see, it is impossible to talk about any one of these elements without referring to the others, because they are all interactive and interdependent in the improv process. It takes a combination of elements to produce a coherent, entertaining, meaningful improv scene.

ACTIVITY—THE OTHER ELEMENT

Whichever elements become the focus of the scene, they can always be enhanced by "activity," that is, doing something physical. Activity takes the situation beyond simply "talking heads" speaking dialogue to action-motivated behavior. The execution of an activity tells a lot about a character and will lead to exploring new avenues of the plot and the environment.

Suppose the scene is about falling in love at the laundromat. A woman could be having trouble getting the washer to work. A man pretends he knows what he's doing and tries to fix it for her. She lets him think that she thinks he knows what he's doing and they fall in love. That's pretty simple, but it shows that, because of an activity in the environment, the premise if fulfilled. The environment and plot bring the characters together, but the action—his trying to fix her washer—gives them an opportunity to interact. The continuation of the activity throughout the scene will provide a forward motion to the plot. The characters' relationship can build as he gets closer to fixing the washer.

BEGINNING, MIDDLE, AND END

Every scene has a beginning, a middle, and an end. That may sound obvious on the surface, but in a good scene the beginning should lead to the middle, which will lead to the end. A well-constructed scene has a certain symmetry to it. Certain things should be established up front, explored and dealt with in the middle, and rectified in some way at the end. The audience must receive enough information at the top of the scene to understand what is going on. They need to know whom they are watching, where they are, and what they are doing. This exposition is known as "setting the scene." Since an improv scene is not very long, this setup should to be as brief as possible. The job usually can be accomplished with a sentence or two and/or a well-defined attitude or activity. Be careful not to tell too much while laying out the exposition.

The exposition at the top of the scene depends on the information the audience has supplied in the suggested premise. How you choose to use that information gives you control of the scene. Withholding certain information intentionally can add mystery to the plot. The climax of the scene might reveal someone's identity or where the scene has taken place. One time at Off The Wall the audience suggested "talking on the phone." The scene began with someone sitting in a room chatting away on the phone. Numerous other calls kept coming in, but the person kept putting everyone on hold. Finally someone entered and revealed that the person busy on the phone was a suicide-prevention operator. Lights out. Not knowing who or where the person was set up the ending.

Consider this structurally balanced, fleshed-out version of the laundromat scene: The guy could be leaning up against a washer reading a book. He glances up and, by moving his head in a circular motion, we discover that he is watching his clothes tumbling in the dryer. His focus is then drawn to the door as a young woman enters carrying a large basket of laundry. We can tell that he is attracted to her by the way he looks at her, and, as they make eye contact, she shows a coy interest in him. This beginning of the scene establishes the characters without so much as a word being spoken.

She puts her laundry in the washer, puts in the quarters, but the machine doesn't come on. She tries everything, but it won't work. The guy sees his chance. We now have a plot developing and we're into the middle of the scene.

Even though he has no idea what to do, he offers his assistance. She accepts, so he goes to work on fixing the machine and getting to know the girl. Just as he gets her washer whirling, they enter the ending portion of the scene.

They now look into each other's eyes as he backs away, feeling very proud, and goes to take his own clothes out of the dryer. His smile quickly fades as he pulls out a sweater that has shrunk to the size of a small child's. Holding the sweater up to his chest, he says, "Gee, I guess I left this in a little too long, huh?" He has endeared himself to the girl. The audience laughs. The end. The lights fade out.

He didn't have to get the washer working. Scenes are seldom all tied up neatly by the end. The conflict doesn't always have to be resolved. Though, some conclusion should be made, even if it is that there is no conclusion. The general rule is that once the premise has been fulfilled, the scene may end at any time. The last line of a scene, the line that ideally gets the laugh or ties it all together, the line that makes the lights go off, is known as the "button," the "tag," the "blow-off," or the "closer." If the line is not funny, it should at the very least be conclusive.

The scene need not necessarily end with a funny line. The lights might go out on a "sight gag," something visual that makes the audience laugh. It might be a facial expression or a physical gesture of some kind. In the case of the shrunken sweater at the laundromat, it is the imagined visual of the tiny sweater and the performer's ability to make the audience see it that gets the laugh. That type of performance is referred to as "space work," meaning your ability to handle an imaginary object and give it space. The technique is very similar to pantomime, although it seldom involves walking into the wind. It does involve defining an object like a door, a window, clothing, or a drinking glass. Anything that you wish the audience to see must be defined by your use of it.

BE SPECIFIC

The use of details or "specifics" is recommended in all elements of improv comedy. Humor comes from specifics. So, whether you are attempting to find humor in a person, place, or thing, be specific. This attention to detail is what makes an improv scene more interesting and potentially funnier. Whether you are planning to perform improv or to write scenes, train yourself to look for the specifics in a situation. Things like what kind? what size? how many? what color?

Pick a noun. Then think of various adjectives you can put in front of it. This exercise will help you to think of specifics. Try to come up with an adjective to attach to each noun in some way that seems interesting to you, that tells a story. Make every generality a specific. The word "chair" is not particularly interesting, but add the adjective "electric" and suddenly you have a story element. "Tree" doesn't really draw a picture, but "giant tree" does. A wallet is a wallet, but make it a "stolen wallet" and there is the beginning of a plot. "Blue cow," "wrong number," "dribble glass," even "used car" draws a much more vivid picture than simply "car."

An improviser needs to be able to think about several things at once. Your primary focus has to be "in the moment." You have to be listening to what is being said and aware of what is going on around you at every moment. But, at the same time, you also need to be considering your options for the rest of scene—what direction your character will take, how the plot will evolve, and how the environment can help you accomplish these things. As you do this, you will also need to be coming up with specific things that are funny about the situation. There's simultaneously a lot to think about.

THE FOUR BASIC RULES

There are four basic "rules" I feel are necessary to follow when learning to improvise. Because improv is spontaneous by nature and you are trying to break new ground through creativity, there will be times when you stretch—and perhaps even break—these rules. But in the interest of learning, I suggest that you follow them until you feel experienced enough to know when you can get away with manipulating them to your advantage.

DON'T DENY

Improvisation is based on building upon what is already given (such as a suggested premise, a line of dialogue, or a scene that has already been set up), accepting it, and taking it one step further. Denial is the opposite of that. Denial is disputing something that has already been established. It's usually a result of either not listening or refusing to give up a preconceived notion of what is going to happen next in a scene. Once something is established, you can't change it unless the change becomes a way of furthering the plot.

A scene should continually move forward. Each new line or action should further the story. Denial momentarily stops the action. When you deny what has previously been established, everything comes to a halt while you figure out which information is correct. You must deal with each piece of information as it evolves. Improv is a series of adjustments. Each line builds on the previous one, and each action has a reaction.

If the scene is a parent/teacher conference and the teacher says, "Your son Johnny has been causing a disturbance in class," and the parent responds, "I don't have a son named Johnny," that's a denial. The intention of the parent may be to avoid taking responsibility for his son, but it comes across as a denial of the information already established by the teacher.

There is a fine line between denial and conflict. Conflict is the interaction of people with opposing points of view on a particular matter—like whose turn it is to do the dishes. One character says to the other: "It's your turn to do the dishes tonight, I did them last night." It is denial and does not further the scene to respond: "No you didn't, I did them last night." All this can lead to is an argument of: "No you didn't." "Yes I did . . ." A more effective response might be: "I know it's my turn to do the dishes, but since I cooked dinner every night this week, maybe you should take an extra turn." In that way you are not denying the statement, but you are maintaining the conflict and are furthering the scene by opening a whole new area for discussion.

Here is an example of something that seemed at first like denial but actually became the hook for the scene. The audience suggestion was "giving up a friend." Archie Hahn did the scene with me as a guy who was about to tell his best friend that he didn't want to be friends anymore. His reason was that I wasn't a good friend. He began by asking me how many years we had been friends. I said fifteen. He said no, we had been friends for twenty-five years. At that point it seemed like denial. But he immediately justified it by saying that if I had been a good friend, I would have remembered how long it had actually been.

The plot twist is a device that might appear to be conflict but is not. Something that appears to be one thing and later turns out to be something else is not denial. An apparent stranger, for instance, may turn out to be your long-lost brother. A detective investigating a homicide may later turn out to be the murderer.

SHOW US, DON'T TELL US

Improvising is acting. Don't just say how you are feeling or what you are doing, act it. Instead of saying something like, "I'm feeling awkward . . ." show the awk-wardness through your activity and dialogue. Show us by being hesitant in expressing yourself, having difficulty in being assertive, or perhaps being prone to clumsiness. This behavior will convey your awkwardness much more effec-tively than just talking about it. If your character is angry, don't say you are angry, be angry. If the audience is going to be told everything that happens, they might as well just read the scene instead.

PLAY THE MOMENT

Since everything you are doing is being made up as you go along, it is absolutely necessary to play a scene moment to moment. If you are able to think ahead at the same time, that's great, but your first priority should be what's going on in the present. Every line is dependent upon the previous one. Each moment should lead to the next. Each action should have a reaction.

Listening is one of the most important factors of successful improvisation. Even in a scene about two characters who are either unable or unwilling to communicate with each other, like a couple having a spat, the actors must be completely in tune with each other in order to express their characters' lack of communication. Two characters on stage, each doing his own thing independent of the other, will never produce a coherent scene. You can't be so busy thinking about what you are going to say or do next that you miss what is going on in the moment.

PLAY THE SCENE LEGITIMATELY

Be real. You can't separate good acting from good improv. This isn't meant to restrict what you can play. You can be as bizarre as you want. You can be as extreme as you want. You can play anything you want. As long as you treat anything you do on stage as reality for that moment, the audience will believe it. You can become a toaster if you want to, as long as you behave like a toaster would in the given situation.

The great thing about improv is that there is no limit to what you can play. The options are endless. The fact that there are no sets, costumes, or makeup takes away all the restrictions. The more experience you have, the more you become sensitive to what an audience finds funny and what you as an improviser do best. While you can use the workshop to practice your strengths, you should also be overcoming your weaknesses. Improv is all about trying something new.

NO JOKING PLEASE!

Is being funny the goal? If you are performing improv comedy, I'd have to say yes . . . with a resounding qualifier— BUT NOT AT THE EXPENSE OF THE SCENE! Humor should come out of the situation and characters, not in spite of them. A joke or some piece of schtick that interrupts the flow of a scene can be ultimately damaging to the piece as a whole, no matter how big a laugh it gets. That laugh will be forgotten by the end of the scene anyway if the piece, as a whole, falls apart from misdirection. Now don't get me wrong. Jokes are great. After all, you are performing comedy. Just make sure the joke is organic to the situation, rather than something funny that you say to get a laugh, whether it fits the scene or not. If a scene is made up of just a bunch of jokes, it probably doesn't have much substance to it. *The best improv scene is one that has outrageously funny dialogue derived from well-drawn characters who are playing out a fascinating, thought-provoking situation.* Good luck achieving all these things at once, but that should be your goal.

Students in my workshops are sometimes dismayed, insisting that they just don't think funny. Can a person learn to think funny? Everyone has the instincts, but some are more developed in this area than others. You can learn the skills to implement these instincts at the right time. You can also learn to recognize where the potential for humor is and learn to express yourself in a way that will enable others to share your sense of humor. It's true that some people just think funnier than others. Some people immediately see the humor in any situation. But, expressing the humor in a situation and making jokes are two different things. It is not your ability to make jokes that will ultimately make you a successful improviser. It helps, that can't be denied, but the primary source of humor will come from the situation and characters.

A funny line or action will often be the result of how—and when—it is performed. "Timing"—when a line is delivered or an action is performed—is ultimately important. A line or an action that may be funny at one moment can completely lose its punch a moment later. Similarly, dialogue or a "piece of business" (a physical action) that has nothing inherently funny about it may play hysterically when performed by an appropriate (or inappropriately appropriate) character in the right situation. No matter how funny your ideas may be, you must learn when and how to initiate your humor.

Wendy Cutler, an improviser I have worked with for many years, almost never makes a joke. She will seldom say something that can be quoted later to get a laugh. But she is one of the funniest improvisers I know—and one of the best—because she completely throws herself into her characters and plays each scene moment to moment.

People generally laugh at two things: familiarity and surprise, something they can relate to and something that catches them off guard. Though they are opposite concepts, they both inspire comedy. Familiarity refers to the common life experiences that we all encounter but that we don't often deal with in an open, honest way. The ability to point out and make fun of these universal feelings, like the awkwardness of a first date or the pressures of dealing with our family, make wonderful subjects for improvisational comedy. Humor from familiarity also involves pointing up some observation or activity most of us have commonly experienced, like trying to steer a grocery cart with a broken wheel. I have had great success by pushing a chair on stage as if it were a grocery cart and having it insist upon moving only in a circle as if one of the wheels were stuck in that turned position. It's funny because so many of us have encountered the same problem. People will also laugh at something they know is coming because they are pleased that they thought of it, too.

Comedy from surprise works by leading the audience in one direction and then switching on them at the last moment, catching them off guard. For example, I do an East Indian character who speaks with a thick accent. Once, when asked where he was from, he responded by asking, "Originally?" "Yes," said the interviewer. "Cincinnati," he answered. This got a big laugh because it was totally unexpected. The clarification of "originally" misled the audience, who of course expected him to say some city in India.

Improv comedy is a very different theatrical form than stand-up comedy, even though they both often deal with the same subjects. If you are performing stand-up, telling a joke out of context that has nothing to do with anything else is perfectly acceptable. When performing an improv scene, that kind of joke can interrupt the flow of the plot. Don't try too hard to be funny. Don't try to make jokes. Let the humor come from the characters and the situation. Some stand-up comics have difficulty working with other performers because they will try to fit jokes, perhaps from their act, into a scene when they aren't appropriate to the flow of the story. With practice, however, stand-ups can become wonderful improvisers because they have already trained themselves to look for the humor in a situation.

If you are going to make a joke, the audience shouldn't know in advance that the line is going to be funny. Don't telegraph the punchline. To be the most effective, the part of the line that makes it funny should come as close to the end of the sentence as possible. That way the audience is more surprised. Playing Ted Koppel one night at Off The Wall, Tom Tully said, "President Reagan spoke today before the Veterans of Foreign War Films." It's a funny line, but it wasn't a joke until you heard the last word of the sentence. Until then, it sounded perfectly normal. The joke would not have worked if he had said, "The Veterans of Foreign War Films were addressed today by President Reagan."

The use of certain subject matter will almost always get what is referred to as a "cheap laugh." Anything to do with sex or bodily functions falls into this category because of its shock value. People are surprised when you say something on stage that many of them would never consider saying out loud in the privacy of their own home, much less in front of an audience, so they respond by laughing. Just saying the f-word will usually get a cheap laugh, so it's up to you to have some integrity in your choice of material.

My policy on "dirty" material is that it has its place. Sex is as much a part of life as anything else. It's something we all can relate to. It's a subject that is important to people, so why not deal with it in improv? If you treat sexual subjects the same way you treat any other subject, you should do all right. Be judicious. Try to make an interesting choice. Use innuendo. Try to make a point. Use the subject sparingly. You wouldn't make every scene be about cars, so don't make every scene be about sex.

If you're not sure, wait to let the audience introduce it first. You're taking suggestions, so let them have the choice. But remember, one suggestion is only representative of one member of the audience. Keep in mind that once you introduce dirty material into a show, it's hard to go back. Sometimes when an audience realizes that you will do that kind of material they don't want to hear anything else.

Many successful comedians have made frequent use of the language and subject matter in question. Sometimes you need to be extreme or even shocking to get people's attention. To me, it's not the language that's important, it's the message. Lenny Bruce and Richard Pryor made very insightful observations while incorporating some of the roughest language of their times. Andrew Dice Clay, on the other hand, gets attention with his language, but once the audience is listening, they hear only a man who is for some reason often predisposed to degrading others.

I do discourage frequent use of diseases, afflictions, and bodily functions as subject matter, but each person has his own sense of humor and people can find comedy in virtually anything.

Sometimes, in an attempt to keep a scene from "dying," when it is not working at all, an improviser will break the reality of the scene by making fun of the scene itself, or a fellow actor, or—maybe if he's really desperate—by making fun of himself. After all, many of us grew up watching Johnny Carson make fun of his own monologue if it wasn't going well. He tells a joke and, if it gets a laugh, he goes on to the next joke. But if it doesn't get a laugh, he sometimes bails himself out by calling attention to the fact that it didn't get a laugh. He improvises, depending on the audience's reaction. Sometimes a large portion of the humor of his monologue comes from him covering for the jokes that aren't working. He's a master of that technique. The difference is that you are already directly addressing the audience in a stand-up monologue. When you talk about one of your jokes, it becomes part of the act. In an improv scene, you have created the illusion that you are characters in a location rather than performers on a stage. By calling attention to a scene's failure, you break that illusion and therefore destroy the scene's characters. In the case of an improvised scene that isn't working, it is better to use your energy and wit trying to save the scene's life by taking it in a new direction. You might try to:

Explore a different area of the situation.
Use the environment to find an activity.
Add conflict.
Develop your character.
Find a motivation to change your attitude.
Hope somebody else enters with a great idea.

Stay in the reality. Bailing out by calling attention to the scene's weaknesses is nothing more than an admission of failure, even if it does get a laugh.

Note: There is difference between a workshop and an actual performance. In spite of all your good intentions and playing by the rules, funny is funny. A room full of people laughing is a wonderful thing. When an audience pays to see a comedy show, they expect to laugh, so it may occasionally be appropriate to break some of the rules to keep the comedy coming. The workshop is the place to learn to do it right. Stick to the rules and try to work your way out of a rough situation. But during a show . . . (more about this in the Performance section).

LEARN FROM OTHERS

There's no better way to master improv than by doing it, but you can also learn a lot by watching others. One Thursday night when Off The Wall was still at the upstairs dance studio on Fairfax Avenue in Hollywood, a guy came into the workshop wearing a baggy, brown, double-breasted suit and a colorful round cap. When he got on stage, he spoke with an authentic sounding Russian accent and referred to a small book as if it were a Slang American Dictionary. Then he launched into a myriad of characters with lighting speed until we were all stricken with a sense of awe as well as pain from continuous laughter.

Our director at the time, DeVera Marcus, asked him to join the performing company the next night. We were fortunate to have the then-unknown Robin Williams as a member of Off The Wall for the next year and a half. We all learned something from watching and working with him. The thing about Robin, aside from his enormous talent, is that he enjoys performing so much. He loves it. He can't wait to get onto the stage. That enthusiasm rubs off on the audience. Performing should be fun. If you're having fun, the audience will have fun watching you.

Andy with Robin Williams, 1978. (Photo by Rick Barnes)

TWO

THE ELEMENTS

CHARACTER

CHARACTER IS WHO YOU ARE

I have worked over the years with many very talented improvisers, all of whom are funny in their own unique way. More often than not, the ones that prove to be consistently interesting and entertaining are those who have built a repertoire of characters from which they can draw at a moment's notice. It's a gift to be able to come up with funny things to say, but one can learn to be able to say things in a funny way. A comic is defined as a person who says funny things, whereas a comedian is known as someone who says things funny. An improviser who relies solely on his wit is forever under pressure to come up with his next funny line. But an improviser who has spent time creating a number of well-drawn characters has built a foundation for his comedy upon which dialogue and action can come to life.

Playing a character does not necessarily mean that you are playing someone much different than yourself. You may, but you don't have to. Pee-Wee Herman is a character that Paul Reubens plays. Fernando is one of Billy Crystal's many characters. Gilda Radner would become Roseanne Roseannadanna. The legendary Charlie Chaplin usually appeared as the Little Tramp. These characters are obviously much different from the real-life actors. They all become their characters by changing their voice, their physical appearance, and their attitude to create an entirely different persona. If you are going to play multiple characters—like Billy Crystal, Jonathan Winters, Lily Tomlin, Dana Carvey, or Tracey Ullman do—taking on these extreme character traits is necessary to distinguish between them. It is not necessary, however, to make such great adjustments to create a funny and believable character.

You can essentially play yourself in a variety of different roles determined by the attitude you adopt at the time. By playing yourself, I mean that you need not take on a character voice, like an accent or other affectation. You may play someone your own age, your own nationality, and your same physical type, but you adopt an attitude that will convey the point of view of the person you are portraying.

The character that Woody Allen plays in his films is essentially the same from film to film, even though he plays a different role in each film. Whether playing the role of a writer or a revolutionary, the character is that of a neurotic Jewish intellectual. His attitude is a combination of confusion, inquisitiveness, judgment, and paranoia. Woody Allen may or may not be like that in real life, but he takes on that persona when he becomes that character.

Becoming the character is the key. Once immersed in a character, it seems to take over. If you have done proper preparation, the character takes on a life of its own, reacting and speaking accordingly, whatever the situation. I have found myself saying things and even using certain vocabulary while in character that I would never have thought to use as myself.

Suppose you are in a scene where a policeman pulls you over for speeding. As yourself, you might feel awkward about trying to talk your way out of a ticket. But suppose you become the character of an escaped convict who has a million dollars waiting for him on the other side of town if he can get there in time. Now you have an entirely new frame of reference. You certainly have a strong need to get away from the policeman who pulled you over. You also probably have no qualms about lying through your teeth. As the convict, you'll do anything you can to get the hell out of there. So don't think about what you, the actor, would say in the situation, think about what the character of the convict would say.

There is no limit to the kinds of characters you can play. You are in no way restricted to your own size, nationality, race, or even sex. But, whether your character is as extreme as an effeminate German wrestler with a limp or as simple as a construction worker who is afraid of heights, the important thing is to play the character legitimately. You must become the person you are portraying, not a cartoon version of him. Play the role, don't role play.

You cannot separate good acting from good improv. A funny voice and funny lines are not enough. Playing an improv character requires the same skills as those used in acting a legitimate role. Yet, improvisational comedy is often based on exaggeration. How do you exaggerate and play it legitimately at the same time? This is achieved by establishing a character that is based in reality. Once an audience accepts the reality of the character, you are free to deal with its extremities.

Archie Bunker can make an outrageous ethnic slur and get away with it because his character is an established bigot. But Edith Bunker making the same remark would be wrong because we know that it would be out of character. You can go as extreme as you want, as long as the character you're playing believes everything he is doing and saying and everything he is doing and saying is appropriate to the character.

The elements of familiarity and surprise—the two things that seem to make people laugh—are also very valuable in creating characters. The audience will enjoy watching you play a character that they can relate to, someone about whom they can say, "I know somebody just like that." You want to avoid playing a stereotype, however. You want to try to capture the essence of a character, not just the shell. The way to give your character individuality is to invest part of your own personality into the character. Find what it is about you that is completely different from anyone else, and use this to make your characters unique. This, combined with "playing the moment" and dealing with the particular situation of the scene, will take you beyond the stereotype. Your character should live a life on stage, not just imitate one. Familiarity is a good place to start when creating a character, but surprise the audience by showing them how your character has a mind of his own.

It is especially satisfying to create a unique character, a personality with whom the audience is unfamiliar and whose behavior is a surprise. This doesn't happen very often, but when it does, it is a truly inspired moment. Dana Carvey's Church Lady from "Saturday Night Live" is an example of this. She's unique. We haven't seen anyone like her before, but we believe she can exist. Whether your character is your version of a type of person we all know or someone unique, it is ultimately important to play it real. Two actors playing the same part can both do a fine job yet play it very differently from each other. They will each bring a part of their own personality to the role. For instance, Axel Foley, Eddie Murphy's role in *Beverly Hills Cop*, would have been an entirely different character had Richard Pryor played him.

A character that many improvisers like to play is the "nerd"—the loser, the wimp, the inept. Each actor plays him differently because each bring brings his own uniqueness to the character. Let's face it, everybody has a little bit of nerd in them. So, there are as many nerd characters as there are improvisers.

Woody Allen's nerd character, for instance, is very different from, say, Chevy Chase's. Both have played nerd characters that have trouble impressing girls, are awkward, and are their own worst enemy. But each has their own individual style. By bringing their own personalities to the role, each actor creates his own persona. It's the same thing with improv.

The nerd character has many variations: an intellectual, a clumsy bungler, a painfully shy wallflower. These are all good choices, all legitimate, but you should pick one that suits you. If you are good at physical comedy, you may choose the clumsy bungler. If you are particularly adept at turning a phrase, you may play a better neurotic intellectual.

A character you create can be appropriate for many different situations. His job or avocation may change depending upon the scene suggestion, but his basic personality stays the same. Select situations that will bring out the humorous elements of his personality. Find the vulnerability or the strength of the character and put him in situations that challenge his strengths or weaknesses. An intellectual working at a construction site is funny because he is out of his element. A clumsy surgeon is a humorous choice because he's totally inappropriate. You prepare the personality and then simply allow it to behave when thrown into a given situation. The more characters you have, the better prepared you are for whatever situation arises.

I do a nerd character by the name of Herman Dultz. I have used him in a myriad of situations, from an awkward first date to a beanbag-chair salesman to the person that installs snooze alarms on clock radios. Each time, the character is exactly the same. He just finds himself in various situations, dealing with various conflicts.

HOW TO DISCOVER CHARACTERS

A character may be inspired by a real person you know or have observed, like a relative, someone at work, or a friend from school. You need not necessarily do an imitation, but a trait or mannerism of the person may inspire you. You can hit on a certain quality that makes the person interesting. A character may also be a compilation of a few different people.

People watching is a wonderful way to discover characters. Places like shopping malls, airports, flea markets, and bars house a wealth of interesting characters to observe. Check out people's idiosyncrasies—the way they walk, the way they talk, how they deal with others. Engage people in conversation. Just overhearing something someone says can give an entire impression of the person.

Many people habitually use catch phrases in their speech. Consider a woman who starts every sentence with "Listen, darlin' . . ." or a guy who who can't finish a sentence without saying ". . . don't you know." Those kinds of phrases might express a sense of insecurity about the person. They need reassurance that they are being listened to. A catch phrase can also act as the character's calling card and is often the basis for what the character is all about. The Church Lady always shows her disapproval with the phrase, "Isn't that special." Lily Tomlin summed up her little girl's ideas with, "And that's the truth." Jon Lovitz as The Compulsive Liar made great use of, "Yeah, that's it, that's the ticket." The audience begins to enjoy the catch phrase and looks forward to hearing it.

The catch phrase can also be a good way to key into a character, to help find the voice or attitude or even physical attributes of a character. Practice saying the catch phrase in character. Note how you feel when you talk that way. How does it change the way you physically hold yourself? What is your attitude about life? Saying the phrase will help you to be able to go directly into that character in the future.

ATTITUDE

Every character must have an attitude, a point of view. The stronger it is, the better. Even if the attitude is that of ambivalence, it must be played with conviction. Attitude helps determine your goal in the scene. Your attitude may change during the course of a scene, as may your goal, but the attitude you are playing at the moment will determine your action and reaction.

A character's attitude may be the basis for his humor. A funny point of view will render funny behavior. Jack Benny was a master of the funny attitude. The actual words he said were not particularly funny. It was the attitude with which he expressed himself that made him one of the greatest comedians ever. He was forever incredulous, so a simple "Well . . ." would elicit an enormous response.

Jay Leno has very funny material, but he also delivers his lines with an attitude. It's a "can you believe it?" attitude that punctuates everything he says.

Attitude is the backbone of a character. You can don a hat or glasses to help convey a look, but the real guts of the character are defined by his attitude. How does he behave? Is he sarcastic, manipulative, needy, polite, supportive? You should always be able to describe your character with an adjective or two that explains the way he behaves.

Let's say you want to play a character who is angry. He is angry and unhappy and takes it out on others. Let's give him an appropriate name and occupation. We'll call him Kurt Undercut and have him manufacture barbed wire for a living. With nothing more than that, you can begin to see the humor in the character. Whatever the situation, he will be complaining and sarcastic but, because he is clearly unhappy himself, he will not come across as a totally offensive character.

The exercise Change of Emotions (see page 175) allows you to experiment with all kinds of attitudes.

VOICE

You don't need to talk in a funny voice to be funny, but it can help. If you have a funny attitude or have funny things to say, chances are you are going to be funny. But not that many improvisers have the gift to be able to say funny things all the time, so it helps if you can say things in a funny way. A character voice can help accomplish this. It might be an accent, a speech pattern, a vocal rhythm or pitch, or an ability to mimic someone that makes the improviser fun to listen to.

When Billy Crystal's Fernando character says, "You look marvelous!" the words themselves aren't funny, but the way he says them is. Robin Williams has very clever things to say, but his ability to quickly change characters makes him so much fun to see and hear. The main thing that determines his change of character is the change in his voice. Just "doing" a voice is not portraying a character, but it can be a place to begin.

Experiment with different voices. You can mechanically manipulate your voice by doing things as simple as constricting your throat a little, closing off your nose, or jutting out your jaw when you speak. When you hear people with unusual voices, try to figure out what makes them talk that way. (Not right in front of them, but try to imitate the way they talk later.)

ACCENTS

Some people have a natural ability to speak with various accents. Others can learn. Dialect books, tapes, and records are available that will teach you to speak with regional and foreign accents. Actually listening to a person who has the accent you're trying to master, though, is invaluable for learning the idiosyncrasies of the particular dialect, its sentence structure, and slang.

There definitely are points for accuracy. It is painful to listen to someone do an accent poorly. I highly recommend practicing by talking out loud to yourself in the car or in the shower. Performing the voice or the accent on stage, in front of people, though, is the test. Experiment in workshop. That's what it's for. Try to work with someone who is already proficient at the accent you are learning to do. Let him speak first in the scene, then you can mimic the way he is speaking.

Accents done for comedy are often overstated so as to parody the dialect. An audience is impressed with an improviser's ability to do an accent, but they will laugh at an exaggerated use of it. You can use a very thick accent as long as the character is played legitimately. The accent must be the reality for that character. As Latka Gravas, Andy Kaufman created an accent. He even created his own language. But first he created a believable character. Once the audience bought the character, they bought the accent.

Another humorous aspect of using an accent is the inherent misuse of the English language. Substituting inappropriate words or confusing syntax is generally a good source for a laugh. Once again, it must be believable. The character must be attempting to speak correctly. He should not be aware that he is using the wrong word or phrase.

GIBBERISH

Speaking in unintelligible, nonsensical words that sound like real words is doing "gibberish." There is English gibberish and foreign gibberish. You may wonder, if it is unintelligible, how you can determine the language. The gibberish should sound as much like the language as possible. That's what gibberish is—pretending to speak a language you don't really speak. Faking it. You should actually be trying to make sense with your gibberish. The best way to do that seems to be to think in English about what you are pretending to say in gibberish. You may even throw in a few real foreign words if you know some or an occasional English word disguised as gibberish, which can be funny as well as useful in getting your meaning across. Using gestures, inflection, and tone will also add comedic effect and help communicate your meaning to your fellow actor and the audience.

LANGUAGE

The language of a character can be a determining factor in his personality. Remember how Carroll O'Connor as Archie Bunker often used the wrong word at a very meaningful moment? He didn't just misuse words at random. His mistaken pronunciation or word usage would cause his statement to take on a whole new meaning, usually revealing his prejudice about a situation.

Your language should be appropriate to the character you are playing. The words a person speaks reveal a lot about who he is. Vocabulary is an indication of education and intelligence, or the lack of them. Use of certain words and phrases can determine age and birthplace. A punch-drunk boxer, for instance, is going to have a different vocabulary from a pompous college professor. An old man is going to describe something differently from a sixteen-year-old surfer dude.

When creating a character, take the time to learn some terminology appropriate to the character. Using the correct language will make the character much more believable and real. Besides, the more knowledge you have of a character or subject, the more information you have to deal with in a humorous way.

PHYSICALIZATION

Another way to begin creating a character is through physicalization. You can express a great deal about your character through movement, especially the way you carry yourself. A confident person walks with authority—upright, with long strides, head held high. An insecure person has a certain amount of reservation in his step, looks around a lot seeking approval, proceeds cautiously, tries to hide. Some improvisers find that the character's voice leads them to his physicalization; others find that moving a certain way will help inspire a vocal quality.

A character's age is also defined by movement. Obviously, old people move more slowly than younger ones. Children usually have an abundance of energy. They don't sit still for very long, squirming in their seats. It seems their limbs are always moving.

You can express a great deal about plot and environment as well as character through physicalization. The biggest mistake of beginning improvisers is the tendency to talk too much in a scene. They feel the need to say everything that is going on. SHOW US, DON'T TELL US! The audience is more perceptive than you think. Let's say a woman is on stage alone. She looks in a mirror and fixes her hair and makeup, maybe practices a provocative pose. She checks her watch. She looks out the window. She fluffs an imaginary pillow on an imaginary couch. From these "pieces of business," we can tell that she is probably at her home, expecting someone who seems to be late, and that she wants to make a good impression when that person arrives.

The works of the silent-film comedians are a great lesson in physicalization. They told a whole story without any dialogue. Through facial expression, gestures, and body language they were able to convey exactly what they were thinking and feeling.

The cast of ABC's late night comedy special "Completely Off The Wall." Left to right: Nancy Steen, Andy Goldberg, Paul Willson, Susan Elliot, Rod Gist, Tony Delia, Wendy Cutler, and special guest John Ritter. Dee Marcus is not pictured. (Photo by John Livzey)

PLAY TO THE TOP OF THE CHARACTER'S INTELLIGENCE

This doesn't mean that you can't play a character less intelligent than yourself. It means that a character you are playing should never say anything stupid or naive on purpose. The fact is, if an ignorant person says something stupid, he doesn't know it's stupid. If he did, he wouldn't have said it in the first place.

Norton, Art Carney's character from "The Honeymooners," was not a bright guy, but he genuinely believed everything he said. That's why he was funny. Reverend Jim from "Taxi" is another example. The most absurd things in the world came out of his mouth, but he was speaking from what was reality for him. He didn't expect an incredulous reaction to what he said. To him, his logic made perfect sense. He had genuine naiveté, so the audience bought the fact that he was really like that. The same is true of Woody from "Cheers" and Rose from "The Golden Girls." They're not stupid, they just misunderstand what's going on around them.

In playing a character, you want to show the humorous side of the person, not exploit him. It's a fine line. The determination for staying on the right side of the line is truth. Avoid the cheap shot. It's easy to make fun of the type, or race, or nationality of a person by exploiting the stereotype. But good satire comes from portraying a unique individual who has opinions and values and believes what he is saying is true.

Play to the top of the character's intelligence. The performer should never make fun of the character he is playing. The audience will laugh at a character's ineptness as long as it is unintentional. If something stupid is said or done on purpose just to get a laugh, you can bet it won't. The way to make your character genuine is to play him legitimately. Bill Dana used to play a classic character named Jose Jiminez. Once, when playing a skin diver, Jose was posed the question, "Would you say skin diving is dangerous?" to which he *seriously* replied, "Skin diving is dangerous." It got roars because of his delivery. Jose genuinely thought he was doing what he was asked. He wasn't trying to be a smart-ass. His sincerity got the laugh. If he had delivered the same answer sarcastically, it wouldn't have been nearly as funny.

Play to the top of your character's ability. Even if a character is not good at something, he should always try his best. Applying for a job, trying to impress a girl, auditioning for a part in a play are all examples of situations in which a character might be inept. But for the character to be real, he must always give his best effort. If it so happens that his best isn't good enough, he will come across as inept, but no one is inept on purpose.

IS YOUR CHARACTER LIKABLE?

A character should either be likable or he should be the butt of the joke. Archie Bunker was likable—even though he was prejudicial, selfish, arrogant, and made fun of others—because, in the end, he always proved to be the fool. The same was true of Ralph Kramden of "The Honeymooners." A character can't be mean just for the sake of it.

You can sometimes make more of a statement by playing an unlikable character because you hold the person's negative traits up for ridicule. Playing an unlikable person who is eventually proven wrong makes a statement about him.

At Off the Wall we do a structure based on "Nightline" that involves playing characters connected with a current controversial issue. The audience response is amazing when one of us plays the role of a generally unliked real person such as Saddam Hussein or Manuel Noriega. When we open up the questioning to the audience, they take out their hostilities on the character.

In the classic melodramas, the audience would thrill at booing the villain because in the end they knew that the hero would come in, foil the villain, and save the day. Any "bad" character must have a tragic flaw. For comedy, the tragic flaw should be funny, say a thief who is forgetful. He steals all kinds of great things but then can't remember where he put them, so he never gets to enjoy the fruits of his bad deeds.

ꞌCHARACTER NAMES

A lot of improvisers like to name their characters. It helps to give them more of an identity. The name itself may be funny in that it gives some insight into the character. The names of some of the characters I play, for instance, are Red Neckman, Beef Hunter, and Herman Dultz. You can get an idea who these guys are just from their names. Having names for your characters is also a great shortcut when performing improv with a troupe. In the brief moment you have before starting a scene, you can quickly alert your fellow performers to what character you will be playing by simply mentioning his name. They can adjust accordingly and perhaps play an appropriate counterpart.

CREATING A CHARACTER
FROM SCRATCH

Even if you are uninspired, you can create a character systematically. Pick an occupation, one you know something about. An improv actor must often know more about the kind of part he is playing than an actor with a script because he is writing the character's lines as well as performing them. It is advantageous to know the ins and outs of the subject at hand. Should you find yourself at a disadvantage, though, a good tack to take might be to play ignorance, such as an apprentice, a novice, or a child who is forgiven for not knowing anything about the subject. Your lack of knowledge in a subject might lead you to play an inquisitive or puzzled character in the scene.

Most people know something about shoes, however, so let's take the occupation SHOE SALESMAN as an example. Now give the character an attitude. How about AMBITIOUS. He will try anything to make a sale. And PROUD. He takes pride in knowing his shoes. It's fine to combine two attitudes. It gives the character more dimension. And now a name . . . we'll call him HERMAN—and let's say he's a bit of a NERD and talks with a NASAL QUALITY to his voice.

Let's set up a scene where HERMAN can do his thing. Put him in his own environment, the SHOE STORE, and give him someone to play off of. Let's say a WOMAN is buying a pair of shoes. In this case we want to explore Herman's character, so the woman will play a supporting role. She should have an attitude that will create a conflict for him, support his character by playing to his weaknesses. Set him up by putting obstacles in his way. Let's say she's an upper-class matron who is a hard sell. She can play the attitude of stubborn.

```
INT. SHOE STORE - DAY
A WOMAN IS WAITING AS SALESMAN HERMAN BRINGS
HER SEVERAL PAIRS OF PUMPS TO
TRY ON.
```

                    HERMAN
This pair is a size six. I know you
requested a five, but they run small.

                    WOMAN
What color is this?

                    HERMAN
These are mauve. I know you requested
beige, but I think you'll find these
equally as versatile.

THE WOMAN TRIES UNSUCCESSFULLY TO FIT INTO THE
SHOE.

                    WOMAN
Don't you have beige?

                    HERMAN
The thing about mauve is that it is the
center of the indigo-violet family. It's
equally at home with your blues as well
as your reds.

                    WOMAN
The dress I want the shoes for is brown.

                    HERMAN
                 (persevering)
Oh, well, we have many brown styles.

                    WOMAN
I want beige.

                    HERMAN
                (getting another shoe)
Well, I have this one with a slightly
higher heel.

                          WOMAN
          It's too high.

                          HERMAN
                    (getting desperate)
          You could take this white pair, and
          dye them beige. I can recommend a
          very good shop.

                          WOMAN
          I need them tonight.

                          HERMAN
          This particular mauve actually goes
          quite well with brown...

   Now let's take the same scene setup and turn it
around, explore the character of the woman, and have the
salesman play the supporting role. Let's say she's a RODEO
RIDER from Texas who talks with a thick DRAWL. She's
OUT OF HER ELEMENT, having never bought a pair of high
heels in her life. Her attitude is SPUNKY. We'll call her LILA.

INT. SHOE STORE - DAY
LILA IS TRYING ON A PAIR OF THREE-INCH PUMPS.
SHE CAUTIOUSLY TAKES A COUPLE OF STEPS.

                          LILA
          Whoa,these are rougher than a bucking
          bronco. This oughta be a blue-ribbon
          event.

                          SALESMAN
          You have to get used to them.

                    LILA
How much do these go fer?

                  SALESMAN
Those are one-twenty-five.

                    LILA
One-twenty-five! Not much leather fer
the money.
          (indicating her boots)
I paid a hundred fer these and they
come clear up my calf.

                  SALESMAN
We carry boots as well. Would you like
to see some?

                    LILA
Nah, I'm going to a fancy dinner
dance. Wearin' a gown. Sides, I
already got me a pair a boots.

                  SALESMAN
How about something with a shorter
heel?

                    LILA
No, I'll ride these. I can break 'em.
You got any socks to match?

With the same basic setup, we have created an entirely different scene because of the characters. The environment, the shoe store, remains the same. The buying and selling of shoes is the activity in each case. But the plot of the scene changes dramatically depending upon which characters are the focus of the scene. In both cases, the humor comes out of the personalities of the salesman and the customer and how they deal with the situation. Their attitudes and manner motivate their dialogue and behavior.

When you are given a situation, such as shopping for shoes, you need to make some quick decisions as you begin the scene. Who are you? What kind of shoes are you looking for? What is your attitude about shopping? If you have a character already prepared in your repertoire, you're ahead of the game. The character of Lila takes over and reacts appropriately to the given situation. The same applies to the suggestion of selling shoes. Who are you? Do you like your job? Are you good at it? Plug in Herman and a lot of the questions are already answered.

You can use Herman or Lila in any number of situations. Herman might be any kind of salesman that's called for, or he may be a guy on a date that happens to be a shoe salesman. In any case, though, he is proud and ambitious and a bit of a nerd. If you play those attitudes, they will always give you a direction to go in the scene. Lila will always be a spunky but simple girl who grew up on a ranch, alien to city life. She is also appropriate for many different scenes and situations.

PLAYING STRAIGHT

In both of these example scenes, one character was dominant over the other. In the first scene, the woman played what is called "straight" for Herman. In the second scene, the salesman played straight for Lila. The straight person leads the scene by moving it forward, setting up something for the dominant character to respond to. They wait for the response and then take the situation one step further. Playing straight doesn't mean that you avoid being funny, but your primary job is to keep the action moving.

This role is just as important as that of the dominant character, for, without the straight person, there is no one to respond to.

Another example would be a scene of an eccentric doctor treating a patient. In this case, the more normal the patient is, the better because his normalcy makes the doctor's eccentricity more absurd. The straight character provides a counter balance to the more "crazy" character. If they are both crazy, then crazy becomes normal and it's no longer unusual.

You can also reverse the situation. The doctor could be the normal one and the patient could be the eccentric. In this case, find an unusual problem for the patient and the doctor can play straight for him.

A classic kind of straight person is the "interviewer." His role is to ask appropriate questions that will "set up," that is, lead the character toward funny responses. Carl Reiner used to interview Mel Brooks as the 2000 Year Old Man. Brooks got all the laughs, but he couldn't have done it without Reiner.

Again, though, the opposite can also work. When Billy Crystal plays his character Fernando at Fernando's Hideaway, he is the interviewer, the role traditionally of the straight man, but his character is so strong that he is the funny one. The guest becomes the straight person, providing a forum for Billy's comedic reactions.

It is possible to have two strong characters in the same scene, as long as they work together to build the scene. When you have two strong characters, they are generally either parallel characters or opposites. Parallel characters are two people who are generically the same, like two nerds (on a first date) or two old people (on a park bench). Opposite characters could be a virgin and a prostitute or the class president and the class clown. The parallel characters can create a slice-of-life-type scene. Opposite characters might conflict, and the scene will be about that conflict. Parallel characters can also be opposite in their attitudes. In the case of the two old people on the park bench, one might be fed up with his life, waiting to die, while the other has every reason to keep on living and loves every moment he has left.

Then there is the type of scene sometimes referred to as "geeks amuck." This is a situation that involves several different dominant characters gathered together in the same location. An example of this might be a psychiatrist's waiting room, where four people are gathered for their respective appointments. Each is a character that the audience gets to know as the characters get to know each other. The scene is about the interaction between the characters. This is a difficult situation to pull off. Four characters on stage at once must always listen to each other, give and take, and avoid talking over each other.

This scene can be helped by adding a neutral character, a straight person that the other characters may react to. At Off The Wall, we often include a structure we call Night School. We take a suggestion from the audience for a course in which adults might enroll for night school. One actor plays the teacher and several others play the characters of the students. The teacher plays straight, acting essentially as a moderator, greeting each student, getting to know them, and providing a structure for the class. This gives a focus to the scene and makes it easier for each character to develop.

You can see that a scene may comprise many different combinations of dominant character and straight roles. In doing improv, you will be called upon at different times to play both. In either case, the same process applies. The four concepts should still be followed. *Play the moment. Don't deny. Show us, don't tell us. Play the scene legitimately.* When a scene fails, it's usually a result of ignoring one of these concepts.

You should always be working at creating new characters. If a situation arises that is perfect for a character you already have in your repertoire, go ahead and use it. But don't get lazy. Don't keep repeatedly going to the same characters because they're easy. Quite often a premise will trigger an idea for a new character that you have not previously tried. Or maybe you have a germ of an idea for a new character, perhaps a voice or an attitude or a physical mannerism that you would like to experiment with. If a situation seems appropriate, enter the scene with whatever portion of the characterization you have so far and let the rest evolve as the scene does. You will discover the character as the audience does. This does not mean that halfway through a scene you can suddenly affect a French accent or arbitrarily change your age. You can, however, start a scene as a French schoolboy and see where it takes you.

ANYTHING CAN HAPPEN, AND WILL

You must always be prepared for the unexpected. You are usually not on stage alone, and you never know what another actor might throw your way. You must be prepared to adjust your character at any time. Remember, you don't want to deny, so if something is established that prevents you from playing your character the way you had planned, you must be open to change.

One actor should never determine another actor's character for him, unless it is agreed upon before the scene begins. In other words, if you are on stage in a scene and another actor enters the scene, don't greet him with "Hi, Uncle Bill!" before he has a chance to speak, unless it has been agreed upon beforehand that he will play your Uncle Bill. Always wait to let the other actor establish who he is. The role he is bringing to the scene is up to him.

If by chance you are labeled, it then becomes your job to fulfill that role. You may enter a scene intending to play a French schoolboy, but, before you can establish yourself, another actor refers to you as the school principal. Like it or not, you are now the school principal. That's why they call it improvisation.

Throughout this chapter we have discussed many ways to prepare realistic, well-drawn characters. But sometimes you are called upon to play a scene that you have no idea how to approach—you are simply not inspired at all. None of your characters seem appropriate. You may not even have an attitude in mind as you walk on the stage. Don't panic. Just play the situation. Determine who you are, that is, what your function is in the scene, and allow yourself to play each moment as it comes. Another actor in the scene may have a approach in mind, so it is your job to follow and be supportive of that goal. As the plot begins to unfold, you discover how your character can help to build the conflict of the scene, and your attitude will evolve.

STAYING IN CHARACTER

You must remain in character throughout the scene. A common mistake is to drop out of character when you are not speaking. As soon as you drop character, the reality is gone. You are no longer playing the scene; you are only an actor on a stage. If your character is not talking, you should be listening, listening in character, reacting, gesturing, walking, thinking as your character would.

Staying in character makes it much easier to think of something to say. You know you have a good character when he takes on a life of his own. He begins to speak for himself. Playing an improv scene is reacting naturally as your character would. A well-developed character should have defined temperament, intelligence, morality, and even political affiliation.

DIALOGUE

Since an improv stage setting is generally neutral, and costumes and props are kept to a minimum, the two main ways of communicating in an improv scene are through action and dialogue. That is, what the characters do and what they say while doing it. "Dialogue" is the lines that are spoken in a scene. While dialogue is the most common means of establishing information and providing humor for the scene, it is essentially the result of the other elements. Who and where the characters are and what they are doing in the scene should inspire what they say.

Some beginning improvisers seem to think that dialogue is the only ingredient of a scene. I have often seen improvisers who are given a scene suggestion simply stand in the middle of the stage and talk. They neglect to establish any character, environment, or plot. They simply try to think of funny things to say about whatever is the given subject. This is essentially joke writing. There's nothing wrong with jokes, but if you allow dialogue to evolve naturally from characters acting out a situation, then you are creating an improv scene and the jokes can be woven into the characters' dialogue. The jokes should be part of the story. If you commit to the character and play the reality of the moment, then the humor should come naturally. By exactly focusing in on who a character is and on his attitude in the situation, you open yourself up to know what the character might say. It sounds trite, but you become the character.

Your own personality doesn't have to be anything like your character's to be able to imagine what he might say. You just have to put his head into yours. If you become that person in that situation, then you just say whatever you imagine you would say were you that person in that situation. If you can also zero in on what things could be funny about that person being in that situation, then you will improvise funny, but believable, dialogue.

As I said before, some people just have a knack for coming up with funny lines. With experience, you can learn to "think funnier," but the ideal, of course, is to be able to combine both talents: to create well-defined, believable characters and to be able to supply them with witty dialogue.

Dialogue is particular to character. The kinds of things that a character says depend upon who he is. What is funny out of the mouth of one character is not necessarily funny from another. Similarly, a line that may not be particularly funny in itself can be funny when delivered by an appropriate or appropriately inappropriate character. Your timing—when you deliver a line—is ultimately important. A line may be funny one moment but lay flat a moment later. A line is usually funny because it plays off of another line that has been said just before it. The first line is the "setup." The funny line is the "punchline."

A line of dialogue can also be funny because it plays off of something that has been "set up" earlier in the scene. At Off The Wall, Paul Willson did a character of a Xerox repairman auditioning for a Broadway musical. When given an imaginary "side," a portion of the script to read, he complained that it was light. The director, Tom Tully, said he was sorry that it was such a small part. "No," explained Paul, "the copy is light—it looks like your machine needs toner." This very funny line set up a running gag for the rest of the scene. Each subsequent auditioner, when handed their side, took one look at it and complained they could barely read it.

Nancy Steen, an alumna of Off The Wall who is now a successful television writer/producer, refers to improv as "3-D writing." When you are performing improv, you are writing on your feet, making up the script as you go along.

Nancy's partner, Neil Thompson, an original member of the Los Angeles improv troupe Funny You Should Ask, told a great story about himself and Michael McManus, an extremely talented television and film actor who is also an original and current member of F.Y.S.A. The two of them had an audition for the producers of "Taxi" for a new sitcom about a law firm called "The Associates." At the time, a finished script for "The Associates" wasn't available, so the actors were asked to read a scene from a "Taxi" script. Neil and Michael were in the outer office waiting to be called in when the casting director came out and recognized them from Funny You Should Ask. She asked if they would improvise a scene rather than read from the "Taxi" script (which wasn't really accomplishing the goal anyway). They came up with the premise that two lawyers had just lost their first case together and were blaming it on each other. As Neil modestly tells it, they got lucky and got the room laughing, but they didn't get the parts. Instead, they were asked to become "punch up" dialogue writers for "Taxi." The producers felt that as improvisers they would be able to put themselves into the characters of the show and to create appropriate dialogue. Apparently they were right. Neil and Michael took the job and worked there for the rest of the season.

PERSONAL PROPS

Traditional theater regards "props" as items that are handled by the actors. The improvisational theater discourages the use of real objects that are handled because it is limiting. Since you want to have the freedom to create anything in an improv scene, they are also impractical. You would have to have an unlimited amount of props available. As soon as you introduce real objects, you start to limit the imagination. The existence of some real things makes it harder for the audience to accept something that is not real. The theory is that if nothing is actually tangible, then anything can be introduced.

Improv theater does make use of "personal props." This refers to personal clothing articles that help define a

The original cast of Off The Wall, 1975. Left to right: Judy Pioli, Dee Marcus, Wendy Cutler, Joie Magidow, Andy Goldberg, Chris Thompson. (Photo by Rick Barnes)

character such as a scarf, a hat, a sweater, a jacket, eye-glasses, or a cape. Personal props are ones that can be worn. I suppose that they are actually costume pieces, but they have always been referred to as props. A versatile garment that can be worn in different ways, depending upon the character, is a good prop. An example is a bandanna handkerchief. It could be used as a:

- Handkerchief for a cold
- Robber's mask
- Victim's gag
- Blindfold for "pin the tail on the donkey"
- Pirate's headwear
- Pretty boy's ascot
- Cowboy's neckerchief
- Bob Dylan's headband
- Jewish Grandmother's babushka
- Hanging man's noose

or anything else you can think of.

ENVIRONMENT

ENVIRONMENT IS WHERE IT'S AT

The environmental aspect of an improv scene comprises its setting or location and the general appearance, visible features, and items inherent to that location. Every scene must have a setting of some kind. The characters have to be somewhere. I know that sounds obvious, but beginning improvisers often forget to think about where a scene is taking place. Or, if they do take location into consideration, they fail to make it clear to the audience or their fellow actors.

I asked two students who had just played a scene together where they thought it took place. They had two different answers. They never made reference to it in the scene, so neither one realized that the other had a different location in mind. This lack of attention to environment had shown through in the scene work.

Of the three main elements of improv, environment is the one that is the most violated and/or neglected. As soon as you speak in a scene, you begin to establish character, and whatever you talk about becomes plot. In fact, every time you speak you are influencing and using character and plot. Establishing and using the environment requires more conscious choices. It also requires the most imagination and can draw some of the most vivid pictures.

ESTABLISHING ENVIRONMENT

Establishing the environment for the audience as well as for yourself and for the other actors should be accomplished as early into a scene as possible.

There are many ways to establish environment. One way is through activity. Use the location. As an improviser, you must be able to visualize where you are, because, in most cases, you are working on an essentially bare stage. The classic improv setting provides only a few chairs or stools. It is up to you to "see" whatever location you are in and to make the audience see it as well. Remember, show us, don't tell us.

When establishing a location, deal with as many of the specifics of that environment as you can. The more specific you are, the more vivid a picture you create for the audience. You must be aware of, and make the audience see, space, temperature, objects, walls, doorways, windows, furniture, appliances, props, animals, landscape—anything that is appropriate and useful in making the environment come to life.

A great deal of environmental information can be established without uttering a word. Your attitude and activity should indicate the location. Your behavior in a dentist's office, for instance, will be different than when you are in your own home.

To establish that you are in a dentist's waiting room, you might pantomime reading a magazine, anticipate something unpleasant, and nervously look around as though in unfamiliar surroundings. The audience may not immediately know exactly where you are, but they'll get the basic idea. You can then further enlighten them by subtly rubbing your jaw as though you have a toothache. In ten seconds you have established the location and who you are without saying a word.

If the scene takes place in your living room, you might indicate this by sitting comfortably relaxed, feet up, watching TV.

Generally, the first actor on stage for a scene is responsible for establishing the location. If a scene takes place in an office, the first actor may establish a desk, a chair, or a bookshelf, defining their proximity with use. By the way you sit on an ordinary chair, you can imply various kinds of seating. Sit forward and upright and it becomes a chair at a desk. Use an imaginary phone and it becomes an office. Put two chairs together to simulate a couch or a bed. Anyone entering the scene from then on must respect those imaginary set pieces and feel free to establish new objects inherent to the environment.

Pay close attention to what has been established so as not to deny it. Once an actor establishes that he is seated behind a desk in the middle of a room, for instance, everyone who enters that room has to be aware of and respect it. You can't walk right through the desk. You can walk around it, you can pull up a chair to it—anything you would do in a real office, whatever your character would do, whatever the premise calls for.

Take mental note of any objects established so you can handle them accordingly. Close attention must be paid to accurately reuse some prop or set piece another actor has previously established.

Use judgment in the things you create and in where you place them. Be practical in what you establish. Don't place a piece of furniture or an object where it might eventually get in the way. Just as you wouldn't put a desk in front of the door at home, don't think that you can do this on stage because the object is imaginary.

Two actors in my workshop once played a scene about a detective coming to someone's home to investigate a murder. They established that the body was lying on the floor, center stage. As his first order of business, the detective constructed an imaginary barrier around the body, which filled almost the entire stage. He then ordered the resident of the house to stay outside the barrier. This, of course, left them practically no space to play the rest of the scene. They ended up ignoring the barrier and walking right through it, breaking the illusion they had created. If you find that something is restrictive, you do have the option of changing it. Try to weave the change into the plot so that it doesn't come off as a mistake. Just stay in character and let the problem be paralleled in the scene.

In the case of the police barrier, if the actors admit they have no place to move, that they have painted themselves into a corner, it comes across as a mistake. But if they attribute the mistake to a character, establishing that the detective is inept, then they can solve the dilemma in a humorous way.

Use the mistake. Interesting staging can be achieved by restricting the resident of the house to the stage's outer edge and allowing the detective to roam freely. This also might dictate the plot. For one thing, it gives the detective the upper hand, unless the resident has easier access to something important on the outer edge of the barrier, perhaps a weapon or something else that only he knows is there. Remember to play it legitimately.

Some locations are more difficult to establish than others. You may require a certain amount of dialogue to make it clear where you are. However, you want to avoid the "Here we are in sunny Spain" syndrome. This results when an actor enters a scene and literally announces where he is. Holding a one-sided telephone conversation is a way to establish the setting if you are on stage alone. For example, an actor sitting at a desk and saying into a phone, "Mr. Smith, you need to come down to renew your driver's license" will let the audience and his fellow actors know that he is working at the DMV. Turning to another actor on stage and saying: "I'm here to renew my driver's license" will accomplish definition of location as well as character and plot.

Suppose you want to establish that you are in a bar. You can let the audience know by going up to an imaginary bartender and saying, "Hey, what a nice bar!" But a more interesting alternative would be to casually check the place out, saunter up to the bar, and aggressively order a drink: "Double scotch, straight up!" This choice is more economical because, in ordering the drink, you have not only indicated where you are but have also established something about your character by your choice of drink and by your attitude when ordering it.

Sometimes you may not know exactly where you are when you begin a scene. The location may evolve as the plot develops. That's why it's called improv, because the elements fall into place as they come up. So don't panic. Just listen, play each moment, develop your character, and eventually you will discover where you are and what's going on.

YOU CAN BE ANYPLACE
YOU WANT TO BE

We discussed earlier that anything you want to happen in an improv scene can happen. The same is true for the environment. You can be anyplace you want to be. All you need to do is establish it. The fact that everything is imaginary removes all the limits from what can exist. You can play any character you choose. That character can be any place you want him to be, and anything you want to exist can be at that location. You can be in an ancient tomb with hieroglyphics on the walls. You can be in a space station on Mars. As long as you "see" it and make the audience "see" it, it exists.

Don't be restricted to common locations. Locating a scene in a restaurant or in a room in a house is fine—much of our lives takes place in these locations, so we can relate to them—but too many scenes in the same type of location can get boring. Be aware of trying to make a location interesting and different. A fun scene I recall took place in a living room, but it happened to be in a mobile home. Everything was very compact and within arm's reach. The location became the star of the scene because the humor came from how much stuff there was in such a small space. And since everything was imaginary, such things as appliances, electronic equipment, sleeping quarters for six—things that would normally fill a large three-bedroom house—were readily accessible.

Since no actual scenery is used in traditional improv comedy, the look of the location is left to your and the audience's imaginations. Your job is to convey what is in your imagination to the audience.

Again, the options are endless because there is nothing real to restrict you. You can be

- In a penthouse, able to look down from the balcony at the city below
- In a cave with only a flashlight to illuminate you
- On deck of a cruise ship
- In a cold meat locker
- At the counter of a greasy-spoon coffee shop
- Sharing a common wall and overhearing what's going on in the next room
- In the produce aisle at a supermarket
- In a romantic cabin on a snowy night
- On a factory assembly line
- In the cockpit of a supersonic jet

or thousands of other places, each of which has its own

inherent scenery that can contribute to the overall objective of the scene.

Occasionally, the location can be the punchline for the scene by making the audience think you are in one place when you end up being in another. At other times, keeping the location a secret can develop suspense or a comic twist in the plot. I recall a scene in which the actors began by behaving as children, playing with toy army men. The audience assumed we were youngsters in a playroom. It was then revealed that we were generals at the Pentagon, preparing war tactics.

USE THE WHOLE STAGE

Get used to taking advantage of the entire space that is available to you. Beginning improvisers make the mistake of playing an entire scene standing in a line at the front of the stage. Don't wander aimlessly just to create movement, but, in your mind, decide where specific objects and set pieces are so that you may go to them during the scene. These objects will give you activities to play that will help to build your character and the plot of the scene. Choose and invent set pieces you can incorporate into the story in a humorous way.

Suppose the scene takes place in a laundromat. By establishing washers and dryers, vending and change machines, tables for folding, and a sink, you create a vivid stage picture for the audience and provide yourself with many more choices of how to play the scene. You may also bring objects into the scene in addition to those that you establish as part of the setting. When you enter the laundromat, for instance, you may bring in your dirty clothes, detergent, and a magazine to read. The specific clothes you are washing and your choice of magazine are indicative of the kind of person you are and of what type of lifestyle you live.

You can create an interesting stage picture by establishing another area of the setting just off stage and perhaps even playing part of the scene from that offstage area. Suppose you are a shoe salesman trying to fit a difficult customer. You might have to keep going back into an offstage storeroom to try to find a size and color to satisfy the customer. Each time you return, you have a couple more boxes of shoes with you and are becoming increasingly more frustrated. You may even continue to play the scene from off stage, calling to the customer that you are out of whatever it is they have requested and wondering if some other particular shoe might be to their satisfaction.

I recall doing a scene with Off The Wall when it was at an old dance studio. Several of us were playing children on a baseball field. Robin went out into the hallway behind the audience, as if he had gone out into deep right field. The focus of the audience became split between the stage in front of them and the hallway behind them. This demonstrates great use of the entire space available.

DON'T UPSTAGE YOURSELF WITH SCENERY

Any piece of scenery that you may continually use should be established downstage from where you will be standing. Suppose the scene takes place in a clothing store where you are trying on a jacket in front of a mirror. Establish the mirror downstage from you so that the audience can see you looking at yourself. If you establish the mirror against the side or back wall of the stage, the audience will be seeing only your side or back and will be deprived of your facial expressions.

PROPS

The classic convention of improv is to use real clothing items, such as a hat or coat or glasses, but to leave everything else, including hand props, to the imagination. Basically, if you can wear it, fine—otherwise forget it.

You will only have some of the props you need in a scene, and mixing real props with imaginary ones is confusing. Taking an imaginary hairbrush out of a real purse, for instance, breaks the illusion. So, the absence of all real props makes it easier for imaginary props to exist believably. Of course, your ability to use them is what makes them seemingly come to life.

Using imaginary props on stage is a form of pantomime. An object must be established very clearly and then dealt with as if it is real. Anything you hold in your hand should have mass, weight, shape, and consistency. A drinking glass is a good example. The audience should be able to determine the type of glass you are using by the way you hold it and drink from it. You would handle a beer mug differently than a champagne flute.

When you are finished using an imaginary prop, you must put it somewhere, just as you would a real object. Don't let it disappear into thin air. After using a drinking glass, put it down on the bar or a nearby table or throw it into the fireplace with a romantic flourish, but don't just let it fall to the floor as your arm drops.

ENVIRONMENT AS THE BASIS FOR HUMOR (LOCATION JOKES)

Where a scene takes place can be the basis of its humor. Putting characters in an unlikely setting always makes them more interesting. A premise as mundane as "job interview" can take on a whole new dimension if it is placed in the right setting.

Let's say a person is applying for the job of a secretary to an architect, and the interview is held on the ledge of the twenty-eighth floor of a partially constructed building. Fear would be a good attitude choice for the applicant to play in this case. The prospective secretary should really want the job but be horribly fearful of heights. The architect can further the conflict and action by encouraging the applicant to move about on the beam of the building, perhaps to get him a cup of coffee from the pot located at the end of a girder.

The objects that inhabit the environment are also often a source of humor in the scene. Whether they actually appear and are used or are only spoken of, you should get used to thinking in terms of all the things that can exist in a particular location. Remember that humor comes from specifics.

If the scene takes place in a restaurant, make it a specific kind of restaurant and think of the specific things that might be on the menu. Make up dishes that sound funny to you: Roast Pork with Duck Sauce, Chicken Lips with Gravy. If the you are in a bar, think up funny drinks: Rum and Kool-Aid, Prune Daiquiri. There's nothing funny about ordering "a drink" or "some dinner." The humor comes from being specific and from choosing things that are unexpected or don't usually go together. Fortunately, you don't really have to eat or drink these things.

Get into the habit of thinking in terms of details. Take a lamp, for instance. Break it down into parts. The shade, the base, what kind of lamp it is, what color bulb it has, how you turn it on . . . these are all sources of humor. The base might be a statue of Bart Simpson. It could be a lava lamp. The bulb might be a black light. The lamp might shut off when you turn on the stereo. Anything you think of can exist. Of course, these imaginary things must be described to the audience. You can pantomime a drinking glass, but the only way to let the audience know that it's a Teenage Mutant Ninja Turtle drinking glass is to say so. These kinds of references are essentially jokes, so try to fit them as organically as you can into the improv scene. Jokes are great as long as they enhance a scene rather than misdirect it.

Off The Wall, 1976. Left to Right, back row: Chris Thompson, Marc Sotkin, Judy Pioli, Susan Elliot. Front row: Wendy Cutler, Dee Marcus, Andy Goldberg.

PLOT

PLOT IS WHAT'S HAPPENING

An improvisational comedy scene should tell a story—a short story, mind you, but a story nonetheless. It should have a beginning, a middle, and an end. It should be about something that happens to the characters involved, and there should be a conflict. The story, the unfolding of incidents, is the "plot." Plot is the most improvised element of a scene because it continues to develop throughout the scene. In fact, you don't really know the plot of a scene until it's over. The premise may give you a brief summery of the plot, but the specifics of the story are up to you.

The beginning of a scene should lay out the characters and their relationship, the environment, and the basic conflict. The middle is about the characters exploring and dealing with the conflict. The end of the scene should bring it to a conclusion in some way by either resolving the conflict or concluding that the conflict can't be resolved. This, of course, is a description of a perfect scene. They won't all work out so neatly, but it gives you something to strive for.

CONFLICT

Conflict, something that creates tension in the scene, gives a plot its driving force. It may be a disagreement, an emotional struggle, or anything that poses opposition.

Conflict may present itself in various forms. It may be an issue that the characters disagree on. It may be some unexpected obstacle to overcome. It may be a decision that must be made or a mystery that must be solved. The conflict is what makes the audience care about the characters. They will want to see how the characters will deal with their problems. Whether or not their problems are resolved by the end of the scene is unimportant. What is important is how the problems are addressed.

HOW TO ESTABLISH CONFLICT

The conflict may be established off stage before the scene begins, or it may be discovered as the scene is in progress. This will depend upon the suggested premise— what information the actors are given at the start. In either case, there are many choices to be made.

Here are some examples of premises for scenes that do not include conflict.
- A boy brings home his report card.
- A plumber comes to fix a kitchen sink.
- A first date.

Here are the same basic premises from above, with the addition of conflict.
- A boy brings home a bad report card.
- A plumber goes to fix a kitchen sink and finds out it is in the new home of his ex-wife.

• A first date for two people who have nothing in common.

If the suggested premise does not include conflict, you can add your own conflict before you begin the scene. If you take a moment to confer with your fellow performers before starting, you can establish the information at that time. If you begin the scene without a conference, then the conflict must be determined during the course of the scene. You may, of course, have your own idea for a conflict that you initiate once the scene has begun, but you should be prepared to adjust your idea to accommodate information initiated by other actors.

In any case, the conflict should be established as soon as possible. For the example of the plumber going to fix a sink, a simple choice would be that the plumber is inept. The conflict would then be whether or not he is able to fix the sink. Perhaps the other character is a housewife who knows more about plumbing than he does. Their competition would create the humor of the scene.

The conflict of the scene may, however, have nothing to do with plumbing, as in the choice mentioned above of the plumber discovering he has been sent to the new home of his ex-wife. This is a conflict of emotional struggle, based upon the relationship between the characters. The fixing of the kitchen sink becomes incidental. It provides the activity for the scene. It may help punctuate the conflict, but it is not the conflict itself.

A scene is always more interesting to watch if there is some activity involved. Otherwise, it is simply people in a room, talking. If the dialogue is compelling enough, it can carry a scene, but the addition of an activity will give an impetus as well as a focus to the dialogue. A couple having a quarrel provides conflict for a scene, but a couple having a quarrel while one of them angrily packs a suitcase to leave adds another dimension to the situation. The activity gives emphasis to the conflict.

A scene may involve a combination of conflicts. A plumber may arrive at a house to discover that his ex-wife lives there, and, during the repair process, learn that he is an inept plumber. The ex-wife points out that he was never any good at fixing things around the house. He was inept at everything. The basic conflict is still a divorced couple dealing with each other, but his attempt to fix her sink enriches the emotional struggle.

Sometimes the conflict of a scene is predetermined, built into the premise. The actors are told before the scene begins that a plumber is going to fix the kitchen sink at the new home of his ex-wife. In this case, the actors must discover how they will deal with the conflict. They have any number of choices to make about how this conflict will manifest itself. How do they handle the fact that they used to be married? Do they hate each other? Are they still in love? Is only one of them still in love with the other? Perhaps the ex-wife is now married to someone else. Maybe the new husband is due home any minute. Maybe she's re-married but unhappy with her new husband. Maybe the sink is not broken at all. Maybe she called the company where her ex works, requesting that he make the housecall just so she can see him again. There are always many choices for conflict and how to deal with any given conflict. Once you think of the obvious choice, discard it and then think of a more interesting original one.

When you are required to think of these choices as the scene is unfolding, intense concentration is necessary. As an improviser, you are creating the situation as you are acting it out, so pay attention and remember everything as it is established in the scene.

Don't clutter the scene with unnecessary information or dialogue. Economy is an important element of successful improv. Nothing should be wasted. You don't have much time to build a scene, so it is important for everything that happens in the scene to advance the plot. There is a delicate balance between letting the scene unfold slowly and keeping the action moving. Listen to what the other actor says and build upon it. The exercise "Yes, and . . ." (see page 131) is a good one for learning this process.

STOP, LOOK, AND LISTEN

One of the most important habits an improviser can develop is his ability to listen. Listen first to the scene suggestion. Be clear about what it requires. Listen to whatever is established prior to the scene. If you and the other performers discuss a direction you will take the scene, or determine what characters will be in it, or what you intend to accomplish, then the entire troupe should be working toward these goals upon hitting the stage. If nothing is predetermined, listening becomes even more critical as the scene begins so that you and the other performers can be in sync with each other as you start to establish the plot.

Listen to the audience. Consider their reaction. If they're laughing, then you're probably doing something right. You might want to continue in that direction. Learn to "hold for the laugh," that is, pause to let the audience enjoy themselves. If they're laughing, then they aren't going to be able to hear you talk, anyway. Let the moment peak and then start up the dialogue again as the laughs begin to die down.

A physical activity can be continued during a big laugh because the audience can laugh and watch at the same time. In fact, physical activities such as gestures, facial expressions, or use of imaginary objects can accentuate the humor and build on the laugh.

Listen to and remember the other characters' names so that you may use them later in the scene. This may sound silly, but don't forget to remember the name you give to your own character. I can't tell you how many times I've seen an improviser forget his own character's name when required to repeat it later in the scene.

Watch and make note of everything that happens in a scene. Watch where others enter and note what imaginary objects they handle and where they establish them so that you can further the scene by continuing their reality. You do so by dealing with these objects in the same place and giving them the same size and shape as the other characters.

While you are watching or listening, you should always remain in character. What you see or hear may require a reaction of some kind. If you are in character, you can make that reaction immediate, realistic, and appropriate.

BEATS

A "beat" is a short segment of an improvisational comedy scene that establishes some portion of the plot. (This differs from the "method acting" definition in which a beat marks the beginning to end of an "intention" or a "unit of action.") The improv comedy beat may include more than one activity or idea. Dividing the scene into beats provides a basic outline for the scene. Each beat is a subsection of the beginning, the middle, or the end.

Here's the scene suggestion "a man goes to a doctor."

BEGINNING
Beat 1: The nurse shows him to the room and gives him a gown to put on. She leaves.

Beat 2: The man puts on the gown and explores the examination room.

MIDDLE

Beat 3: The doctor enters and they establish the patient's ailment.

Beat 4: The doctor does an examination.

END

Beat 5: The doctor gives his diagnosis and suggestion for treatment.

The number of beats that make up the beginning, the middle, or the end may vary. The same scene idea might be done in three beats or seven. Also, the same five beats might be done another time by different performers and be completely different. The nature of the ailment, the attitude of any of the characters, what kind of doctor he is, the environment of the examination room, and what kind of exam is given are all variables that will affect what goes on during the course of the beat.

ATTITUDE

The attitude of your character will have a big influence on the plot of a scene. Your choice of attitude will depend on your character's goal. Or, depending on the scene suggestion, you may pick an attitude and see what goal it leads to. Let's say that you are doing a scene in which you are being fired from your job because your work is inadequate. The goal of your character might be to retain his job. You may choose a number of attitudes to accomplish that goal. The goal of your character also establishes the scene's "through-line." The through-line is something that can be stated in a few words and is pursued through the character's attitude.

Let's say you choose to play the attitude of "victimized." Your character thinks he is being wrongly fired, that it is not his fault he is doing a poor job. He thinks he is being asked to do the impossible. Then the through-line of the scene is about whether he is being fired fairly.

Another attitude choice you may make is "desperation." Your character may admit that he is doing a poor job, but he has a sick wife and twelve children to support and desperately needs to keep on working. The through-line would be about his promising to do better if he can only have a second chance.

You might choose to play the attitude of "relief." Your character is thrilled that he is being let go so that he may start working for a rival company. They are dying to hire him so that they can learn some of the production techniques of the current company. This scene might then evolve into the boss changing his mind about firing the employee, even giving him a raise to keep him from going to the competition.

HOW ATTITUDE AFFECTS DIALOGUE

The following is a short exchange from a scene that might take place at the candy counter at a drug store. First, read the lines with no attitude at all.

BUYER: I'd like a pound and a half of red licorice.
SELLER: We only sell it by the pound.

Now read it again with the addition of attitude. Make the buyer shy and the seller sarcastic.

BUYER: (SHY) I'd like a pound and a half of red licorice.
SELLER: (SARCASTIC) We only sell it by the pound.

You can see that the addition of attitude brings the dialogue to life. Now read it again, this time as if the buyer is a seductive woman and the seller is an insecure man.

Now make up more attitudes of your own and read it again. You can see how, with the same dialogue, the meaning can be different depending upon the attitudes of the characters. What direction the scene then takes will be dependent upon those attitude choices.

WHERE ARE YOU COMING FROM?

Your character should always have had a "life" before the scene begins so that your attitude when coming into a scene can be based on something that was going on "off stage" before you entered. This life is usually not something that the audience ever sees. Also referred to as the "backstory," it is a personal history that you make up for yourself to give your character more depth. Giving your character a past will help determine how he will behave and react in the present. Once you begin the scene, you play the moment, but the moment is always influenced by the past. It's just like real life. Any decision you make is influenced by a compilation of everything that has happened to you before that moment. When improvising, your character could have lived any life you care to invent.

From the earlier example of "getting fired," if your backstory includes a fight with a coworker right before you had to meet with the boss, you might try to blame your inefficiency on the other worker. He's the one that should be fired for god's sake, not you. Suppose you had seen your married boss flirting with his secretary. You might use that information to try to bribe him into letting you keep your job.

A fun thing I have seen improvisers do is to let the audience "hear" their immediate past life take place off stage right before they enter a scene. For instance, playing the role of a waiter, the actor improvises a loud, terrible fight with an offstage chef and then enters the scene to take a couple's order for dinner. The waiter may be influenced in various ways. Because of the fight, he might treat the couple badly, taking his anger out on them. On the other hand, he might get a laugh with an immediate mood change, greeting them with a big smile and treating them with the utmost courtesy. This makes for a great running gag, a series of exits and entrances going back and forth between harshly arguing with the chef off stage and warmly dealing with the couple on stage.

DON'T PLAN TOO MUCH AHEAD

Entering a scene with a strong character and attitude is perfectly all right. But be prepared to be flexible enough to alter that attitude should it become necessary. If you enter a scene intending to be a son who is proudly bringing home a report card with straight "A"s, establish that information as soon as possible because, if the father first establishes that you received all "F"s, then that becomes the given. You must then adjust your character's attitude and go with this new information. Find some reason to make your pride appropriate. Perhaps you really are ashamed of your grades, but you are trying to fake pride in the hopes that your father will not look at the report card. You can then make the transition to shame, or fear, or whatever you decide will further the plot and continue the conflict.

WHAT IS IT THAT MAKES A PREMISE FUNNY?

You've made some offhanded comment about something and had someone respond, "That's a funny idea." What is it that makes it funny? There isn't one secret ingredient. There are many reasons why one thing is funny and something else isn't, or why something is funny at one moment but not a moment later.

I don't begin to profess to know how to tell you to be funny. It's up to you to begin to look for what might be funny about a given situation. The subject doesn't really matter. Any subject can be made funny if approached from a funny point of view. Try to think in terms of finding a "hook" to a scene. A hook is some juxtaposition, some reversal, some discovery, some change, some fresh way of approaching a subject. The scene may hinge on some twist in the plot, some irony or coincidence, or something that rings true to life, something to which we all can relate. The character you bring to a situation can also lead to the humor of the scene.

For the structure Night School, each performer chooses, based on the subject, a character and reason for taking the class. They are one step ahead if who they are and why they are enrolled in the class has a funny juxtaposition with the subject matter itself. Some ideas that have worked very well include: Wendy Cutler's character of a French woman taking a French class just so she can feel superior, Bernadette Birkett's character of a nun taking a class about how to flirt, Paul Willson as a man taking an auto mechanics class because he bought a Yugo.

The characters in all three of these instances have a funny point of view, so the performers don't have to rely on trying to make jokes. Their characters' relationships to the subjects will automatically lead them to the humor.

Taking a normal situation and exaggerating it can make it funny. The characters involved may be incidental. In Woody Allen's movie *Bananas*, there is a scene in which he is sent to get dinner for all the revolutionary troops. He goes to a small diner, orders a cup of coffee, and then casually mentions that he also needs something to go. He then proceeds to order 1,000 grilled-cheese sandwiches, 300 tuna-fish sandwiches, and 200 BLTs. Of the grilled cheese, 490 should be on rye, 110 on whole wheat, and the rest on white bread. He also needs cole slaw for 900.

Three things that we have previously talked about make this scene so funny. He takes a normal, everyday situation to which we all can relate (ordering carry-out food) and exaggerates it to the point of absurdity. But his attitude is casual throughout. He treats it as if it is perfectly normal. Since the situation itself is bigger than life, playing it legitimately makes it all the more funny. He is also very specific with his order, even naming the kind of bread. It's a great moment when they bring out wheelbarrows full of cole slaw.

Another example of the situation providing the comedy is an Emmy-winning episode of "The Mary Tyler Moore Show" that dealt with the death of Chuckles the Clown. Chuckles, dressed as a peanut, was crushed by an elephant. Everyone laughs when they hear what happened except Mary, who sees no humor in the tragedy. Yet when it comes time for the funeral, everyone is serious. But Mary loses it and can't keep herself from laughing. Eventually everyone else breaks down with her. The more they all laughed, the more the audience laughed. They played the scene legitimately and let the situation be funny.

Then there's the episode of "The Dick Van Dyke Show" in which Rob had two places to go for Thanksgiving dinner. Having arrived at the second gathering, he doesn't want his host to know that he already had dinner somewhere else, so he forces himself to eat a second four-course meal, even though he's already full. Very funny stuff. An everyday occurrence like going to someone's house for dinner can become very funny if it has the right setup. We know he's full, so we enjoy watching him have to hide it from everyone in the scene.

In these last two examples, a situation is set up in the first act from which the humor of the second act is drawn. This device is used frequently in television, plays, and movies. The audience, primed for what to expect, enjoys seeing it played out before them. Sometimes they even know more than the characters in the scene, and this knowledge gives them some personal stake in the story.

With improv, you don't have the luxury of two acts. There is only one scene, but you can adopt the technique of setting up something in the beginning that you will pay off later. When an improv scene is based on a suggestion, those in the audience who heard the suggestion have some inside information before the scene even begins. If the suggestion involves some specific event, the audience will know the outcome in advance. The humor then comes from seeing how and why it happens.

If the suggestion is "getting fired," we know that eventually somebody has to get fired. The actor knows this, but his character doesn't. So, the character might enter in very good spirits, intent upon asking the boss for a raise. He can then be all the more surprised when he is fired.

Just as the location of a scene can give you a number of areas from which to draw humor, the situation can provide a general theme or subject that will trigger references for comedy. For instance, in a scene about a stewardess making dinner for her date at her apartment, a series of humorous activities can arise if she behaves like a stewardess, even though she's in her own home. She can pour drinks from miniature bottles, serve food on little plastic trays, get her guest a pillow and blanket, and point out the exit in case of an emergency.

Analyzing what's going to be funny to other people is extremely difficult. If it makes you laugh to think of it, then it's probably worth taking a chance on. Of course, what makes you laugh won't necessarily make everybody else laugh, but, unless you are really weird, your sense of humor should be shared by a number of others. Remember, though, having a funny idea is not enough—you must act it out clearly and descriptively enough for the audience to relate to it.

It's like when you tell friends a story about something that happened to you. You think it's really funny but nobody else laughs, so you say, "I guess you had to be there." What probably happened is that you didn't describe whatever was funny about the original situation well enough for your listeners to feel as though they experienced it themselves. When you're retelling an event, you need to be so descriptive that your listeners feel like they are there. When you perform improv, you are acting out the event for your audience. You need to portray the situation descriptively enough for them to feel like they are there.

BEGINNING THE SCENE

Are you on stage when the scene begins or do you make an entrance? Are you doing something as the lights come up? The audience will be looking for clues as to what's going on, so if you don't know, neither will they. You can play it completely spontaneously once you get into the scene, but in the beginning you have to make some quick decisions.

Let's say you have been given the basic premise "a job interview." That's pretty wide-open. The premise doesn't have any built-in conflicts, so you have many options as to how you might choose to play the scene.

The most obvious notion is that the setting is in an office, and one person is sitting in a chair answering the questions of another person sitting behind a desk. Let's go with that. In this case, let's say that you're applying for the job. You need to immediately start figuring out who you are and what kind of job you're looking for. If you have time, think about the backstory of the character—where he is coming from. If you flash on a great idea, all of these things might fall into place very quickly. Then again, you might find yourself sitting opposite the desk with your mind a blank, waiting for the employer to ask the first question. That's okay, too.

If you can, though, come up with at least some element, some area, some approach to the character— perhaps a specific type of job for which you are suited. Attitude is a perfect element to start with. An insecure employer and an overly confident applicant, for instance, might give the situation a comedic twist. The choice of what kind of job you are seeking can also give the scene its humor.

Maybe all you can think of is that you do a convincing German accent and you want to try it. You'll have to improvise the rest. You wait for the interviewer to ask the first question. He asks your name, so you make one up— hopefully, a German name to go with the accent. An Irish name with the German accent would get a laugh, but unless you think you can follow up with a character who is half German and half Irish it's probably not worth the joke.

The prospective employer then asks about your last job. Following the German theme, you might say that you are a Professor of German who was laid off. The interviewer may pick up on your theme by this time and become the character of the manager of Der Wienerschnitzel. He is looking for someone to fill the position of wiener steamer.

Another way to go with the same scene premise might be for the interviewer to establish right away what kind of job is available. Let's say he is a magician looking for an assistant. As the magician, he might put the applicant to the test, involving him in a series of tricks to test his ability and agility. In this case, much of the humor will come from the physical activity.

Basically, whoever speaks first makes a choice of some kind. Anything said in a scene establishes some information about either the characters or the location or the plot. So don't establish anything that you're not pre-pared to deal with for the rest of the scene. Take your time and make your choices carefully.

A common beginner's mistake is to feel the need to promptly establish all the information at the top of the scene. Let the exposition happen naturally. Let the audience discover who and where you are and what your relation-ship is. That's half the fun.

In the earlier example of the plumber and his ex-wife, let us see the tension for a moment before we know why it's there. Sure, the plumber can enter and exclaim, "Alice! I never thought I'd see you again after our divorce. I've really missed you. I heard you got married again." But the audi-ence will have more fun discovering that he is still in love with her and that she allows him to make a fool of himself before she reveals that she has remarried. SHOW US, DON'T TELL US! Let the audience figure things out for themselves. Don't hit them over the head with the informa-tion.

When you begin the scene, you will often have an idea of how you think it should evolve. You should get used to thinking that way, but you should also be prepared to adjust your idea depending upon the direction the scene takes. It may not go the way you planned at all. You must always be willing to give up your preconceived notions, even if you think the way you perceive the scene is more appropriate than the direction a fellow actor has taken it. You can't force a scene to go the way you planned. You must always PLAY THE MOMENT, constantly adjusting as the plot and conflict develop.

FURTHERING THE SCENE

As information is established in a scene, it becomes a given. You cannot negate it. So DON'T DENY! Remember, there is a fine line between conflict and denial. Your character may disagree with another character. He may have an opposing point of view on a subject, but basic information shouldn't be changed. Your job is to take the given information, add to it, and then allow the other actor to accept your new information and build upon it. Through this process, the plot and its conflicts unfold.

Take, for example, the scene suggestion of "a boy bringing home his report card." If the father reads the report card and establishes that his son received an "F" in arithmetic, then there is no denying that fact. The son may have a reason why the "F" is not such a bad thing. He may try to change his father's reaction to the failing grade, but he cannot deny the fact that there is an "F" written on the card. He may even try to convince his father that "F" stands for "Fine" and that he should be proud of him. He cannot however, say, "That's not an 'F,' that's an 'A'." That would be denial. The son's defense of himself is conflict. A denial stops the forward movement of a scene. The scene comes to a screeching halt while the actors try to decide which piece of information is correct. Is it an "F" or is it an "A"? Conflict, on the other hand, builds the scene because it furthers the plot.

A common mistake is the tendency to over-talk a scene. Beginning improvisers feel a need to fill every moment with dialogue, whether it furthers the action or not. Don't be afraid of silence on stage. You've heard the cliché "actions speak louder that words." Just because you're not talking doesn't mean you stop acting. An action, or sequence of actions, or a determined look can speak volumes.

ENTRANCES AND EXITS

When a character enters a scene that is already in progress, he should further the plot. The character should have a reason for entering and should establish it right away (unless for some reason the mystery is important). Don't enter a scene only to linger aimlessly on stage hoping to think of some reason for being there.

The timing of your entrance is extremely important. You must always be listening to and watching what is being established by the actors already playing the scene. If you have an idea that will add to the plot, find the right moment to enter so that you don't interrupt the flow of the scene. Just as you can improve a scene if your entrance is timed right, you can detract from it by entering at the wrong moment.

You generally have to move quickly to enter a scene that's already in progress. It's a bit like entering a turning jump rope. You need to be aware of the rhythm of the scene. If the moment for your idea passes, be willing to give it up. When you do enter a scene, the actors on stage should stop to give you the focus of their attention. They should allow you to establish who you are and why you are there. Of course, if a scene is really going well, there's no reason to interrupt it. Don't intercept your own teammate's touchdown pass.

During a scene in progress, an onstage character may "call" for another character by making mention of him in such a way as to suggest he would like him to join the scene. It is then up to someone off stage to enter as the character referred to. In the plumber/ex-wife example, the ex-wife might say she hears her husband's car pulling into the garage. This is asking for another actor to enter the scene as the new husband. The entering actor should still have the freedom to speak first so that he may establish his character and add on any information he chooses. The actor may enter with something like, "Hi, Honey, I'm home!" so there is no confusion about his role. It is also permissible to recall to a scene someone who has previously exited.

Just because you have entered a scene doesn't mean you must stay there until the bitter end. You have the option of exiting at any time and then perhaps reentering. There should, of course, be some reason to come and go that will further the plot. You should justify your exit by having some task to do or some place to be.

A character's sole purpose in a scene may be to set up some piece of information, plot point, or another character's entrance. This accomplished, he may exit, never to return to the scene again. A basic example of this would be a nurse showing a patient to the examining room to ready him for the doctor. Having accomplished this, the nurse might exit before the doctor arrives. Left alone in the examining room, the patient has a chance to explore the environment and the imaginary props and set pieces.

ENDING THE SCENE

The perfect way to end an improv scene is to resolve the conflict in a clever way, get a big laugh, and have the the lights go off. This, of course, is not always possible. In any case, the lights shouldn't come down on a scene until the premise has been explored. The conflict need not always be resolved. Realization that the conflict cannot be resolved can be a conclusion in itself.

If "buying a pair of shoes" is the premise of the scene and the conflict is that the store does not have the type of shoe that the customer is looking for, then the scene may end without a pair of shoes being purchased. They should, however, at least be shopped for before the scene is concluded.

Usually, whoever is running the lights (improvising in his own right) is responsible for ending a scene. As an actor, you are pretty much at his mercy. So, it is in your own best interest to provide him with an appropriate opportunity. You can lead a scene toward a logical conclusion in hope that the lighting person is attuned to the direction you're going (see Lighting in the Performance section, page 108).

A common way to end a scene is to bring back something that was established toward the top of the scene. A funny remark or action that was memorable from the beginning can be referred to at the end. It may even have been a running gag throughout the scene. Be aware of the comedy "rule of three." Something can be repeated three times and will be funnier each time, but generally it will fall flat when attempted a fourth time.

You need not necessarily repeat an actual line from earlier in the scene. You may continue a comedic theme or reference that has been established. The theme can be used continually throughout a scene. In the earlier example of the date at the stewardess's house, the guy might, having finished dinner, start to make advances toward the girl. At this point, she might announce that he has reached his final destination and that it is time for him to de-plane.

You can, of course, end a scene by having the characters exit the stage, but that should be used only as the last resort. And don't ever walk off alone and leave another actor to finish a scene by himself, unless, of course, you leave him set up for a great joke that will end the scene.

Off The Wall, 1978. Left to right, back row: Andy Goldberg, Wendy Cutler. Middle row: Paul Willson, Dee Marcus, Tony Delia, Susan Elliot. Front row: Robin Williams, Wayne Powers. (Photo by Rick Barnes)

THREE

THE PERFORMANCE

ASSEMBLING A TROUPE

Most of the successful improvisational comedy groups that I have seen or worked with have four to eight members. No matter how many performers you choose to have or what the ratio of men to women is, having a good cross section of performing types is important. By this I mean different physical types as well as people who are adept at various kinds of comedy. You would be well-suited to have, for instance, a "leading man," a "leading woman," and various "character people." With a cross section such as this, you will have an appropriate actor to play whatever type of role a given scene demands.

Leading men and women are usually good-looking in a traditional sense, whereas character people are those who have certain physical attributes that make them distinctive in appearance. This doesn't mean that your leading lady can't play the wallflower sometimes or that your character type can't play the debonair playboy. It's fun to cast against type. But if everyone in the company looks similar, the stage picture isn't as interesting and you won't be as versatile a company.

Usually, an improviser is stronger in one style of comedy or another, and it is helpful for a group to have every area covered. Some people are great at physical comedy while others are clever with dialogue. Some actors are adept at dialects while others have a particular talent for singing or doing impressions of famous people. Having a well-rounded troupe is important so that, whatever challenge presents itself, you have someone who can rise to the occasion.

An improv company must also be prepared to deal with all kinds of topics. Current events, history, science, mechanics, medicine, sales, law, and interpersonal relationships are just some of the subjects that you may be asked to improvise on. Having people with different backgrounds, educations, interests, experiences, and areas of expertise can insure that you will be able to handle any suggested subject.

You will occasionally be asked to deal with a subject that none of you knows very much about. In this case, you must be prepared to fake it. Chances are, if no one in your troupe is knowledgeable of a particular subject, most of your audience will be just as uninformed and won't even be aware of your shortcomings.

WHO'S IN CHARGE?

A big downfall of many improv groups is that they have no director. It is particularly essential when forming a new group to have someone to guide the actors through rehearsals and to supervise creating a running order for the show. Ideally, the director should be someone who is not a performing member of the company, someone who can watch the rehearsals and performances and can objectively give the actors notes. If the director is also a performer, it can be difficult for him to have a clear perspective of the show as a whole, not to mention the difficulty of objectively critiquing his own performance.

It is not always possible to have an outside director. In this case, it is better to have an experienced member of the troupe act as the leader rather than to have no one in charge at all. It is next to impossible for a group of people to make a creative decision, especially a creative group of people, and many decisions must be made when designing an improv show.

Feel free to have group discussions about the format, style, and performances of the show, but allow the leader to make the final decisions. Even if you decide to vote on group policy, allowing majority to rule, you still need someone to lead the vote and enforce the policy. If an improv group has no one to ultimately decide what should or should not be done with the show, then the group will invariably waste a great deal of time and energy arguing over essential creative choices. Even if the leader makes occasional mistakes, a lot of time will be saved. Everyone can be encouraged to make suggestions, but these suggestions should be channeled through whomever is in charge so that the troupe's overall vision of the show will not be lost.

Actors should be free to express any difficulty they have in working with others in the troupe, but these problems should also be filtered through the director or leader. That way they can be addressed in a constructive manner rather than as a complaint from one performer to another.

ENSEMBLE PLAYING

It is especially important that the members of a troupe be able to work together amicably and that each member feels that he or she is an equally important part of the company. There should be no star performer. Everyone should be able to pull their own weight and add their particular strength to the total package. Of course, at any given performance one person may stand out, but each performer should have his moment in the spotlight, so to speak, and the show itself should be structured so that everyone has a chance to do what he does best. The goal is that the entire show be successful. The way to insure a good show is for everyone to work together as an ensemble and not to be concerned with one's own individual performance.

If someone is playing scenes as if they are the only one on stage, it can create a competitive atmosphere that can throw off the whole company. Sometimes, as a defensive measure, others begin to work the same way and soon everyone is vying for the spotlight. There is a difference between taking "focus" and upstaging another actor. To take focus means to have a presence, to be doing and saying something interesting enough to grab the audience's attention. "Upstaging" originally referred to an actor literally standing upstage of the other actors so they had to turn away from the audience to speak to him. It also commonly refers to an actor stealing focus from another by engaging in some distracting activity while the other is speaking. You should learn to be able to take focus when it is your turn, but, when another actor is having his moment, you should be willing and able to be supportive of him. The term for this successful improv necessity is "give and take." Know when to take focus and know when to give it. A little competition can be healthy, it creates energy, but you should get in the habit of playing with your fellow actors and building a scene together.

A performer doesn't necessarily dominate a scene intentionally. It can sometimes be attributed to nervousness. The performer's insecurity can lead him to over-talk the scene. In this case, you can't do much except make the person aware of what he is doing and hope that he will be able to control it in the future.

WORKSHOPPING

The more a company works together, the better they will become. Therefore, as much time as possible should be spent in the workshop. A workshop that's specifically geared toward preparing for a performance will be somewhat different from a general workshop. Time will be spent determining what performance pieces you plan to include in your show. You will find that some exercises are more show-oriented by nature or are, at least, more appropriate to the type of show you are preparing. Repeat these several times to allow everyone to have a chance to try them. This will give you an opportunity to see who is the most proficient at which exercises and will help determine particular strengths of each performer. Alternate working with everyone in the group so that you will feel comfortable when called upon to work with them in the show. It is very important to be able to trust your fellow performers and feel that you are in tune with them. This is accomplished with practice and time spent working together.

The workshop is the place to experiment, to try out new exercises and techniques. Experiment with characters you have never played before. Take the chance to fail in workshop so that your performance can have a better chance to succeed. You can experiment with breaking the rules in the workshop, but be aware of the risk of establishing bad habits.

You might allow scenes to go longer in workshop than you would in a show situation so that you can explore different options and choices. Be willing to go with what another actor initiates. Practice ways to advance a scene. If a scene or exercise doesn't work, take the time to discuss why it failed and then redo it so you can have the experience of it working successfully.

Make use of workshop time also to invent your own

new exercises and scene structures. They may be variations on the ones provided in the Workshop section of this book or all new in their features.

THE SHOW STRUCTURE: PACING AND VARIETY

Having one member of the cast act as a spokesperson or host for the group is a good idea. Before you even begin to improvise, this person can give a short introduction to the show. At this time, he can explain to the audience a little bit about what they will be seeing and what will be expected of them. This will give them a chance to begin thinking of some suggestions so they will be ready when you ask for them later on. The introduction should be brief and friendly but humorous enough to set that tone for the evening.

Keep in mind that many audiences have never seen improv before, so they may be reticent to participate or confused about what kind of things you need from them at the beginning of the show. Let them have a chance to see and understand what's going on and to feel comfortable with the performers before you start asking them for much input. Start by asking for simple ideas. You can build to more complicated suggestions later on.

Properly structuring your show is the first step toward insuring its success. Pacing is one of the most important elements of that structure. When creating a running order of scene structures for the show, consider that the performance should build in momentum as it goes along. You don't want to peak too early, but you also want to get your audience's attention and confidence right away.

Some kind of a high-energy exercise is recommended for the opening of the show, perhaps a group piece that allows the entire cast to be seen. This serves to warm up the performers as well as to introduce them to the audience. Tag scenes or a symphony of some kind (see Workshop section) are good types of opening pieces. By starting the show with an exercise that has a built-in technique to it, you also increase your odds of opening strongly. Be careful not to open with anything too bizarre that might alienate your audience. Do everything you can to win them over in the beginning. Once the audience is on your side, you can introduce more unusual aspects of the show.

The overall style of the show you decide upon should reflect what it is you wish to accomplish in your show. Your goal as a group may be to be politically satirical. You may wish to deal only with interpersonal relationships. You may choose to mix some serious improvisation with your comedy, or you may just choose to provide light entertainment. These are all fine choices, as is combining any of the above.

You may decide that your show will have a theme to it. Perhaps everything will relate to a certain general topic like dating, or life in the '90s, or politics, or family. Anything you choose is appropriate as long as you can maintain it over the length of the show and can approach your topic from enough different angles to keep it interesting and varied.

Variety is essential in an improvisational comedy show. Whether your show revolves around a particular theme or deals with a broad range of topics, you should offer a variety of scenes and exercises. Vary them in length, style, approach, location, staging, and casting.

Whatever the style, the pacing of the show is essentially what keeps it moving. Varying the lengths of the scenes and exercises is the best way to keep up a good pace. Too many long scenes in a row will slow things down. A good rule of thumb is to leave the audience wanting more. Don't keep doing something until they are bored with it. Once a scene or game has accomplished its goal, end it and move on to something else. If one piece goes particularly long, follow it with something shorter. Follow a low-energy piece with a high-energy piece. If something isn't working, try to end it gracefully, as quickly as possible, and move on to something else. If you've just done a two-person scene, follow it with a group scene and vice versa. The more you can vary the show, the more interesting and entertaining it will be.

Varying the location of scenes will help to keep the show fresh in its approach. A simple premise such as "a first date" can take place at any number of different locations. If you just did a restaurant scene, you might set the first date at an amusement park or a drive-in movie or on a miniature golf course. So often, improv groups will set every scene inside a room. This gets monotonous to the audience as well as the performers. Remember that the location will often give you specific activities to play. The more you vary the location, the more kinds of activities you will have available to you.

Location will also help determine the "stage picture," how the setting and characters are arranged on the stage. This is another element that provides variation to your show. Nothing is more boring than watching one scene after another of people sitting in chairs and talking. Learn to use the whole stage. Play part of the scene from the audience area or from off stage if you want to. Don't wander around aimlessly just to be moving, but find ways to take advantage of all the space available to you.

Varying the casting from scene to scene will help to make the show more fun to watch. Don't have the same people working together over and over. A scene may begin with only two actors, then others may make entrances and exits throughout, playing supporting roles to the main characters. The kind of suggestion you ask for can often control the number of characters required for a scene.

It is generally true that improv exercises (see Workshop section) will have higher success rates than premise-oriented scenes. This is because exercises have a built-in humor factor off of which to play. For instance, in Change of Emotions (see page 175), just the fact that you instantly change your emotional point of view in the middle of the action is fun to watch. If you do it in a really funny way, or come up with a great line, all the better. In Playbook (see page 176), if the improvised dialogue played along with the script even makes sense, it's entertaining, so you're one step ahead. It is therefore advisable to "load" a show with enough exercises to help insure a successful performance.

An open or suggestion-oriented scene is more difficult because the actors are responsible for inventing the entire piece—including plot, character, and environment—from scratch. There is no technique to play off of, so not only must the performers come up with an interesting and humorous approach to the premise, they must be able to play it out, creating a beginning, middle, and end.

When approaching a suggestion-oriented scene, consider the many possibilities available. Don't ever let a premise suggested by the audience restrict you. An ordinary premise can be made unusual by playing it in a particular style. Let's say the suggestion is "infidelity." You might play the scene as if it were a soap opera. You might treat it as if it took place in another decade or even another century. A cave man cheating on his wife will give the scene a completely different perspective than if it were a modern middle-class couple. Certain premises can be handled straightforwardly, but don't be afraid to do a scene as if it were a detective novel or a western or even as science fiction.

Keep in mind that you don't have to begin every scene at the absolute beginning of the story. Consider starting a scene as far into the action as possible while still providing enough exposition to set up the premise.

If the suggestion is "having dinner in a restaurant," you can start at any point in the experience, depending upon how you plan to deal with the suggestion. You may begin by arriving at the restaurant, or being seated, or ordering, or waiting for the food to be served. Or you can take the suggestion literally and already be seated, eating, when the lights come up.

If you decide to add to the premise the plot twist that you forgot your wallet, then the humor should really get going when it comes time to pay. Therefore, you might want to start the scene at the end of having dinner, just before the waiter brings the check. A choice that would heighten the conflict would be to establish the environment as a horrendously expensive restaurant where you have had a lavish meal in celebration of a special occasion. Be finishing off an extraordinarily expensive bottle of wine. It will make forgetting your wallet that much more embarrassing. This whole setup can be quickly established with a couple of sentences.

Don't let the audience know ahead of time what the conflict will be. Use the beginning of the scene to set up the expensive and important dinner. The middle of the scene starts when the waiter brings the check and you discover that you don't have your wallet. This is your moment. Your reaction to the dilemma is the basis of the conflict and humor for the rest of the scene. What is your attitude? Embarrassed? Confused? Angry? What are you going to do about it? Make up an excuse? Play dumb? Get pissed? And how are you going to make whatever choice you make funny?

Your character will help determine your attitude. Are you someone who has never eaten in a fancy restaurant before? Are you a regular customer of the establishment? Are you a wimp or a bully? Your character's attitude will help fuel the conflict and the comedy. The location—the restaurant—is spelled out in the suggestion, but the environment of the restaurant is up to you. Is it conservative? Is it dark? Is it ethnic? Are there musicians? Is it owned by the mob?

A lot of the action will depend upon the other characters in the scene—for instance, the waiter and the party with whom you are dining. There are many ways to deal with this situation, but adding the conflict or plot twist of forgetting your wallet gives you a very specific point of view.

Do everything you can to vary all aspects of your scenes to make them as different from each other as possible. You'll have more fun and so will your audience, because they won't know what to expect next.

If you divide your show into two sets (presented to the same audience), make sure that you have two impressive pieces, one to end each set. Your second set may have a different feel to it than the first. By the second set, the audience has had a chance to loosen up and so have you. Once you have won them over and they feel confident that you know what you're doing, you can begin to take greater risks and do more unusual and complex pieces. Be careful, however, not to rest on your laurels from the first set. You must continue to give a good and accessible show. Commonly, an audience will tend to remember most clearly the last thing they saw. A mediocre show that ends well will be remembered more fondly than a good show that ends badly.

WHAT TO ASK FOR IN A SUGGESTION

As you begin to structure a running order for your improv show, you will need to determine what kinds of suggestions you will ask your audience to supply. Guiding and educating your audience about what kinds of ideas are appropriate is important at the beginning of the show. If left completely to their own devices, they will sometimes attempt to stump the cast with ideas they think are too difficult to pull off or make suggestions that they think are funny. In the latter case, the suggestion itself is usually a joke, or an attempt at one, and you are left with no place to go. You want to be challenged and you want the audience to have a chance to be creative, but you want to remain in control of your own show.

You can experiment to find out what questions will get the kind of replies you prefer. This doesn't mean that you want to trick the audience into suggesting certain premises. Make your questions general enough to elicit ideas from which you can build scenes, but specific enough so that you can get the kind of ideas that you feel comfortable with.

Often, the most simple suggestion makes the most interesting scene. A suggestion that is too specific can leave you no latitude for creativity. A simply stated, general idea leaves you, the improviser, the opportunity to come up with a unique way to deal with the premise.

To a certain extent, leading your audience when eliciting an idea is fair game. If, for instance, you have a particular character you enjoy playing, you may ask for a premise that would easily involve that character. Say you play a therapist. You may ask, "What is a reason to go to therapy?" and then improvise a scene with another actor playing a patient who suffers from the suggested problem. Other times you will have a particular scene structure in mind that requires a specific kind of suggestion. Such a structure might be a classroom scene that involves a teacher and three students. In this case, you might ask, "What is a subject you studied in school?" The cast member that knows the most about the subject might play the teacher while the others play students. Or it might be fun if one of the students turns out to know more about the subject than the teacher. In any case, vary the types of students in the class. One might be the teacher's pet, another is a goof-off, yet another might be a foreign exchange student.

When doing an improv exercise, the suggestions you ask for may be very specific, depending upon the needs of that exercise. You may require a list of emotions or several authors or a current event. Sometimes you will simply ask, "Who has an idea for a scene you would like to see?"

IS IT ALL RIGHT TO TURN DOWN A SCENE SUGGESTION?

Some groups do, some don't. Some always take the first suggestion they hear. Some will wait for an idea they like. If several suggestions are called out at once, you can simply pick the one you find the most interesting. Sometimes only one idea is called out, so you're pretty much stuck with it. I personally feel that you should take any idea that is suggested unless you have an extremely good reason for turning it down.

Occasionally you are going to get an audience member who will yell out something just to get a laugh or to impress a buddy or girlfriend. If you find a suggestion distasteful, chances are the audience will as well. There's no need to subject an entire room to watching a scene that they don't care to see to accommodate the one weirdo in the crowd. It's your show, so you should have the last word on what's in it.

If you're going to turn someone down, however, be prepared to do it diplomatically, perhaps humorously, so as not to come off as rude, defensive, or insecure. Let the audience member know that he's off the mark, that you could deal with his idea but simply choose not to. You might say something like, "That's one idea, somebody have another?" You might also ask the audience to vote whether or not they would like to see the scene in question. Of course, you run the risk that they will, and then you have to do it. Refusing an idea should, however, be a very occasional occurrence. The fact that you can't think of a way to approach a premise right off the top of your head is not a good enough reason. That's the challenge of improv. Besides, one of your fellow cast members may have a fine idea of how to handle the premise. So go ahead, take it, and hope for the best.

THE HUDDLE

Once you have taken a scene suggestion from the audience, you should begin to perform that scene as quickly as possible. You may take a brief moment for the group to discuss the suggestion, or actors may simply get on the stage and see what happens. Existing improv groups that I know of seem to be divided between the ones that huddle before the scene and those that just go straight to the stage. I don't recommend one method over the other. I recommend trying both ways and then choosing the one you prefer.

I will say that taking a brief moment to huddle, to caucus, to confer, to brainstorm ideas, or to exchange information will generally result in a scene that gets to the point more directly than a scene that starts from scratch. Without the huddle, you have no idea who, where, or what another actor is playing until you find out in the scene. All you can do is make a choice for yourself and be ready to adjust if necessary. You should, of course, be able to quickly establish those elements for each other and the audience once the scene begins. Keep in mind that a quick exchange of information just before walking on stage can save moments of time and prevent confusion later. On the other hand, planning a course of action in the huddle can sometimes inhibit spontaneity on stage. Needless to say, there are advantages to both methods.

If your group does huddle, then you literally put your heads together to try to predetermine a basic approach to the scene or premise suggestion. Agree on a location or a character or, if you're lucky, a funny plot twist. This, of course, must be a rapid process—I mean seconds—because the audience is waiting. Maybe a piano or guitar player or even a band keeps them entertained, but too long between scenes will break the momentum by slowing the pace of the show.

Suppose the suggestion is "buying a car." All that is provided in this suggestion is an activity. It's up to you to provide the rest of the elements. You can quickly make some choices in the huddle that will get the scene started. Who's buying a car? Who's selling it? Where are they? Is it a new car or a used car? Is it the buyer's first time buying a car? Based on this open-ended suggestion, there are dozens of choices you can make in the huddle. The buyer might be answering an ad in the newspaper and the scene takes place at the seller's home. It might take place at a car dealership where a father has taken his teenage daughter to buy her first car. The scene might begin with a potential buyer taking a test drive with an aggressive salesman. Any one of these specific ideas can be quickly agreed upon in the huddle to give you a head start on playing the scene.

The more experience you have, whether from a workshop or a show, the more easily and quickly you will be able to make choices. You will begin to learn what kinds of things work for you. You will begin to develop your "bag of tricks," a stable of characters from which you can call upon for a good cross section of situations. You don't always have to start from scratch in creating your character for a scene. You may be able to plug in one from your bag of tricks.

With experience, you will also become more comfortable working with your fellow performers. As you become familiar with each other's characters, it will be easier to make choices in the huddle and you will be able to establish relationships more quickly once the scene begins. Knowing what character another performer is going to play will give you a head start in knowing how he might deal with a given situation. Two performers may even develop two characters that work well together and request a kind of suggestion specifically for them. Or they can just plug them in if an appropriate suggestion is made. At Off The Wall, Bernadette and Wendy have characters of a mother and daughter that are used in this way. We might get the scene suggestion "coming home late." In the huddle we just say "mother/ daughter," and they go up on stage and start improvising.

Even if you do huddle, you may not be immediately inspired. No particular idea or character may seem especially appropriate to the suggestion, or you may just decide to go ahead and wing it. Take your time, listen to your fellow performers, keep track of what is established, and build a scene together. Sometimes the most brilliant scenes come with no preconceived information. They are free to develop entirely from the moment.

LIGHTING

The lighting of a show is an essential element of the performance. By lighting, I refer to two different aspects— the illumination of the stage and the determination of when to turn off the lights. The actual lighting itself is often dictated by the physical equipment available to you. If you are performing in a well-equipped theatre, you may have access to an extensive lighting board with many instruments and available choices. In this case, you should use those options and take advantage of the variety of moods and looks you can create with lighting. Spotlights and gels, area lighting, and special effects can spice up a performance. Most comedy clubs' lighting schemes are geared toward illuminating one stand-up comic, so you are forced to make do.

The most crucial element of the lighting, however, is deciding when the lights go off, because this determines the end of a scene. Some improv groups have a non-performer operate the lights; others do it themselves. This decision may be made for you by the physical layout of your performance space. In a case where the lighting controls aren't near the stage, having an extra person is essential. If the controls are near the stage, it is possible for the performing members themselves to run the lights. In this case, whoever is not in a particular scene can take his turn at the switch.

In either case, the person running the lights has a very important job. A scene is tremendously influenced by how and when it ends. Learning when to end a scene is learning to be a good improviser. A great scene can be ruined by allowing it to run too long. It is important, however, to allow a scene to develop long enough to deal with and fulfill its premise in a satisfying manner. The general rule of thumb is that it is better to end a scene too early than to let it run too long. A scene that is allowed to run too long can have a negative influence on an entire show. Always leave the audience wanting more.

Since varying the lengths of scenes will help the pacing of the show, it is sometimes necessary to cut a successful scene short in order to pick up the pace of the performance as a whole. Be prepared to make sacrifices for the good of the show.

Sprinkling the show with strong, short scene, known as "blackouts" will also help to keep things moving. A blackout is a scene that consists of one punchline. Sometimes that punchline is the only line spoken in the scene. Sometimes a short setup is required for the punchline. Good blackouts are difficult to come up with because they must fulfill the premise swiftly and also be funny! A blackout scene must be done as quickly after taking its suggestion as possible because it usually deals directly with the way the suggestion is made, perhaps its exact phrasing.

When you have an idea to deal with a scene suggestion as a blackout, try to give the lighting operator the punchline. A blackout may also be the choice of the lighting operator seizing the opportunity in an appropriate situation. If the first beat of a scene has fulfilled the suggestion and gotten a big laugh, it may be time to turn out the lights. The question becomes: Is it going to get even better? Has someone already said or done what could very well be the funniest thing about the premise? If so, black it out. Even if the scene may get better, it still might be a good time to end it, depending upon the pace of the show to this point. If you've just had a long scene, a blackout might be just the ticket. Maybe you'll miss something that could have followed, but maybe you won't.

Lighting operator is a difficult job. The person is often blamed for something that he has no control over. If the actors run out of material, they wonder why the lights didn't go out sooner. If the lights go out while the scene is on a roll, the actors wonder why the lighting operator didn't let it go longer. Having one person run lights for your group on a regular basis can be extremely beneficial. He will become familiar with the habits and abilities of the performers and be more apt to realize when a scene has peaked. Once the choice is made to turn off the lights, always do it with conviction. Don't ever start to turn off the lights and then change your mind and bring them back up. This will only confuse the performers on stage, who will think that the scene has ended and then be forced to start it up again. You may, however, use a technique called a "fade out" or a "slow fade." When a scene ends with something such as a funny reaction by a character or two characters engaging in a heated argument, it is sometimes effective to let that image linger for a moment as the lights slowly fade; a scene ending with a verbal punchline is usually best accentuated by a quick blacking out of the lights. If possible, have the lighting operator attend the workshop so that he can practice along with you.

Whenever they can, the actors should communicate their game plan for dealing with a sugestion to the person running the lights. Immediately following the huddle, someone who is not going to be in the scene can convey any necessary or helpful information to the lighting person. Perhaps a plot twist has been established in the huddle. Tell the lighting person so he doesn't take out the lights before you get to it. A performer may enter a scene in progress with the intention of bringing it to a conclusion. He may have what he thinks is going to be the blackout line. This is something the lighting person must know. For some reason, a mediocre closing line can be enhanced by having the lights go out. Psychologically, the blackout enhances the effect. Of course, you often have no idea ahead of time where a scene is going, so the lighting person is left to his own good judgment.

If the light controls are in a booth or in the back of the theater, an intercom with headphones can be helpful. Hand signals to communicate lighting cues such as blackouts are sometimes useful as well. I have seen groups who use a signal from the stage to cue the lighting operator to turn out the lights. They use a subtle hand signal that is only apparent to those who are looking for it. I have also seen a switch on the floor that can be activated by the foot of someone on stage. It turns on a small red light at the lighting controls, signaling the operator to turn off the lights. I don't really recommend these systems. They seem to create a delay between when the scene has ended and when the lights go out. In something that is so dependent upon timing, only a short delay can make a difference. I think that you must have confidence in your lighting operator. If you don't, try to find someone else for the job.

"The Other Brothers," David Ruprecht and Andy Goldberg performing with Off The Wall at the Hollywood Improv, c. 1980. (Photo by Coralie Jurick)

MUSIC AND SOUND EFFECTS

Many improv groups use music to enhance their show. Most commonly, a piano or guitar player plays in between scenes and provides accompaniment for improvised musical numbers. When playing between scenes, it is fun if the choice of song is appropriate to the suggestion. For instance, if the audience suggestion is "going to a psychiatrist," the musical interlude might be "Going Out Of My Head."

A musician who is adept at accompanying actors as they improvise a song is invaluable and can add a great deal to a performance. Musical improv requires a special skill and should be practiced in workshop so that the actor and musician learn to follow each other and are flexible enough to go in whatever direction either is led. If live music is not practical, prerecorded music can be used at appropriate times.

If possible, it can be an asset to have an offstage microphone or two available to the members of the group who are not in a particular scene. It can be used for "calling" certain exercises and to provide sound effects or offstage voices for a scene in progress. The onstage performers might be watching a movie or TV show for which the sound can be provided. Offstage performers can use the microphone to provide the sound of a dentist's drill, the engine of a car, a complaining upstairs neighbor, a crying baby, or a voice from the dead at a seance.

IS IT EVER THE AUDIENCE'S FAULT?

It's always easy to blame the audience for a bad show. If a scene or performance doesn't go well, you will often hear improvisers complain that the audience was stupid or gave bad suggestions. Of course, after a great show the performers will invariably comment on the excellent crowd. Interestingly enough, in either case, the audience is referred to as if they were one person with a single personality. Indeed, it does often seem that way. The audience seems to form a group decision about how they feel about the show.

It is your job to entertain and you can't decide that an audience doesn't deserve a good show because they don't appreciate your humor or give you the kind of suggestions you dream of. Sure, you may get a few suggestions that you wish you didn't have to do, but any premise can be dealt with humorously. If a suggestion is undeniably bad, you shouldn't have taken it in the first place.

There, of course, may occasionally be a difficult group within the audience. If you are performing in a nightclub, you will sometimes run across a group within the audience that has perhaps been over-served, so to speak. If they become inappropriately vocal, you may try addressing them in a humorous, forceful, yet non-threatening way, such as, "Thank you for sharing." Unfortunately, if that doesn't work, there's not much you can do about it, short of having the doorman bounce the offenders. Don't give an offensively verbal audience member much attention because you will only encourage him.

Other nuisances in the audience include people who should have just gone for coffee because they are more interested in talking to each other than in listening to the show and the couple who uses the show as foreplay to whatever they have planned later in the evening. Then there's the guy who came to a comedy show to prove to his friends that he's funnier than the performers on stage. Beware also of a large group of people in the audience who have a connection to each other in some way. They may all work together, for instance, and may give suggestions that refer to work-related inside jokes that don't mean anything to you or the rest of the audience. Try not to play only to this section of the audience or allow them to dominate the scene suggestions. If, however, the entire audience is made up a group that all has something in common, you might try to learn something about that common denominator beforehand so you can refer to it during the show.

A good show is always the best way to insure a good audience. Don't let them get away from you. If what's happening on stage is funny and interesting, and if you as performers are enjoying what you're doing, then you can't help winning over any audience members who had an "impress me" attitude when they first sat down. Yes, there are exceptions, and some audiences are better than others, but, for the most part, the cast is responsible for the show's success or failure. Unfortunately, if a show starts out badly, sometimes the performers become self-conscious and stop having fun, which only takes the show down another notch. You have to keep going. The luxury of doing a series of unrelated scenes is that any single one can change the flow of the show. You can be dying a horrible death and then suddenly score with a killer scene—you're back on top of it.

LEAVE YOUR WORRIES AT THE DOORSTEP

Don't bring your personal life with you into the theater or workshop if it's going to have a negative effect on your temperament or your work. You might have had a terrible day or just finished having a fight with your girlfriend or boyfriend. Leave it at the theater door. Even if you're unhappy off stage, you should be enjoying yourself on stage or there's no point in being there. If you just can't ignore the negative feeling, try using it in a scene. Much comedy material comes from frustration, anger, and unhappiness approached in a humorous way. You can't just go on stage and complain about how miserable your life is. But, chances are, if something is bugging you, it will bug other people, too, and they'll enjoy listening to you make fun of it. Plus, you get it out of your system. You should be passionate about whatever subjects you deal with. Much of the theory of acting involves using true emotions or at least the memory of true emotions that you have felt in real-life situations.

HOW MUCH OF AN IMPROV SHOW IS IMPROVISED?

The question I am most often asked after a show is, "How much of that stuff was really improvised?" I say, "All of it." Some of it may not have been improvised for the first time that night, but it was all improvised at one time or another. Characters recur, topics recur, and sometimes lines are keepers. I think you owe the audience a good show, and sometimes you can help accomplish this by sharing a line with them that's really funny (if it's appropriate to the moment), even if you improvised it the week before. The fault lies in forcing a line into a situation it has no place being just because you think it will get a laugh. The fact is, if it's in a place it shouldn't be, it won't play nearly as well anyway. If you find yourself repeating entire scenes over and over, however, then you're not improvising, you're performing sketch comedy.

ORIGINALITY

It is said that there is nothing new under the sun or that everything is a variation of something done before. If you think that way, you will never become a successful improviser. Sure, you're going to cover themes that have been explored before. You're going to create characters that have similarities to characters you have seen other people do. So, your job is to discover a fresh approach to whatever you're being called upon to improvise. Throughout this book, I have given you examples of things that have been done in the past. Use those examples to guide you rather than to limit you. The whole purpose of improv is to be inventive, to think in ways that are new to you.

Originality is an integral part of performing comedy. When people are first starting out, they sometimes have a tendency to emulate performers they admire. If you fall into this category, just make sure that you emulate and don't imitate. You certainly don't want to do someone else's act. You don't want to play someone else's characters. You want to try to cover territory that hasn't been covered before or at least approach it from a fresh direction. It's not as difficult as you think to be unique, because nobody else is you. You have something that no one else has—your own personality and your own life experiences.

The cast of Funny You Should Ask, 1991. Left to right, back row: Doris Heiss, Michael McManus, John Bates. Front row: Hennen Chambers, Phyllis Katz. (Photo by Charles Chambers)

Off The Wall, 1991. Left to right: pianist Carol Weiss, Andy Goldberg, Bernadette Birkett, Paul Willson, Wendy Cutler, Archie Hahn, Tom Tully. (Photo by Marianne Atkinson)

FOUR

THE WORKSHOP

GETTING STARTED

The size of the workshop depends upon your situation. A traditional school classroom may have thirty or forty students in it. A private improv class or an informal workshop might have less. Ideally, the number of improvisers should be small enough that each performer gets adequate stage time yet large enough that there is an "audience" to observe and respond to the performances. Generating comedy is certainly easier when someone is there to laugh.

As in any activity, be it a sport or an art, there are many exercises you can do on your own to strengthen your proficiency. In the case of improv, the exercises used in the workshop are the same as those used in a show. Not all workshop exercises lend themselves to a performance situation, but if you choose to go that route, you can pick the ones you prefer. Personal exercises are included in the improv exercises and scene setups in this section. These are designed for those who don't have a workshop available as well as for those who do to use as additional practice on their own.

The workshop space itself should be large enough to have a "stage area." It need not be a theater per se, but lights focused on the stage area with a lighting dimmer available to blackout the lights at a scene's conclusion is preferable. If a lighting dimmer is not available, one person not in the scene may be designated to end it by starting applause.

The stage area itself need not be too large, perhaps

long enough for at least four people to stand side by side and a few feet deep. Of course, a raised theatrical stage with wings for entrances and exits is an asset if one is available.

Minimal scenery and props are required. A few chairs or stools can serve a multitude of purposes. I recommend that props be restricted to things that can be worn, such as jackets, hats, and glasses. These props, in fact, are used more often in a performance situation than in a workshop, but they can be useful to help "get into" a particular character.

Ideally, the workshop has a leader—someone who is knowledgeable, sets up the exercises, and gives constructive criticism and suggestions at the end of each performance. Since such a person is frequently not available, rotating the role of leader among the most experienced workshop members might be helpful. In this case, the leader need not necessarily give instruction but can at least prepare the game plan for that particular session.

As you will see, some exercises require a leader, or conductor, or caller (see page 127). This role also can be rotated among the members so that each performer has a chance to experience doing the exercise as well as conducting it.

Since the workshop is the place to experiment, to try new things, it must have a supportive atmosphere. When critiquing an improviser's work, it is important to point out accomplishments as well as mistakes. If you are going to criticize something about the work, try to end the critique by also emphasizing something that worked. There will likely be some performers who progress more quickly than others. This should be taken into account during any critique session, realizing that what is routine for one may be a new accomplishment for another. It should also be stressed that the opportunity to work with someone more advanced is a chance to rise to the occasion rather than to be intimidated.

Should a scene be interrupted if it just isn't working at all? This is ultimately the workshop leader's decision. If the performers seem not to have understood the point of the exercise and are going about it a wrong way, then I recommend stopping it. If they seem to get the idea but just aren't executing it well, then whether or not to stop and comment on the problem is a tough call. Perhaps the actors are having difficulty getting to the point but seem like they will soon get with the program.

It can sometimes be beneficial to flounder. In learning what doesn't work, you can direct yourself toward what does. On the other hand, continually performing scenes or exercises that miss the point can be frustrating enough to cause someone to give up. It can also reinforce bad habits. The first time someone makes a mistake, it can be mentioned at the conclusion of the scene. If the mistake becomes a recurring problem, interrupting a scene in progress may be necessary to point out the mistake as it is happening and to suggest an alternate direction. Then just before the improvisers begin work the next time, the leader can reinforce the direction with a gentle reminder. Students must be willing to listen to criticism and learn to apply new-found knowledge to their next attempt.

You don't need to be on stage performing for the workshop to be a learning experience. Much can be learned by watching others and determining what works or doesn't work in their scene. By critiquing and listening to the critique of others, you sharpen your own skills as an improviser. You can be much more at ease to make choices about how you would play a scene when you don't have to be in it, so the practice in making those choices will pay off when you are in the situation yourself.

Though you can learn from watching others, you should never copy another's performance. You can pick up techniques, such as how to creatively use the stage or how to do an accent, but each performer should have his own style. Your unique personality and talents will help determine that style. The workshop is the place to discover and nurture your performing personality and to learn to integrate your talents into the process of improvisation.

THE ORDER AND CHOICE OF THE EXERCISES AND SCENE SETUPS

The following section is broken down into categories—beginning and group exercises, character exercises, advanced exercises, and scene setups—to help those who are designing a lesson plan for an improv workshop. It's not quite as simple as one from column A and one from column B, but a good workshop session begins with a warm-up exercise, then a group exercise, and then a couple of scenes. You should always vary the types of structures you do in a session to keep it fresh and to keep up the energy. An entire session of, say, two-person scenes, no matter how good they are, will become monotonous after a while. Throw in a high-energy exercise each time, an exercise that stresses character or conflict, then maybe a group scene.

You might do a theme session occasionally where the whole time is spent working on one particular area such as character, environment, conflict, or accents. You can still use varying types of exercises and scene setups that concentrate on that area to keep it fun. Sample theme sessions might be

Conflict:

Laughing/Crying (Warm-up exercise)
Change of Emotions (Advanced exercise)
Innocent Bystander (Three-person scene setup)
Patent Office (Two-person scene)

Character:
  Hitchhiker (Warm-up exercise)
  Dialect/Occupation/Emotion (Character exercise)
  Three Through The Door (Character exercise)
  Panel (Group character exercise)

The exercises are listed roughly in order of their degree of difficulty. Beginning improvisers may want to concentrate only on the section of "Beginning and Group Warm-ups" for the first few sessions. Then, when ready, move on to more advanced exercises and scene setups.

Exercises and scenes that can be played with several people at once should be used first, because the more people you have on stage, the less pressure there is on each person to carry the scene. Later on, for more intense playing, you can repeat the same structures with only two people.

Keep in mind, however, that the more people you have on stage, the more difficult it is to give and take. Listening, which is always so important, becomes doubly so when more than two people are in a scene. If you have four people on stage at once, remember that only one can talk at a time and that the rest are actively listening, meaning that they are still in character and furthering the scene but they are giving focus to the person speaking.

If the whole class is going to be doing the same scene setup or exercise, you'll have some advance time to make some choices prior to your turn. Depending upon the structure, there are many decisions you can make. This doesn't mean you should pre-write a scene in your mind, but you can make certain choices ahead of time and still react spontaneously when in the scene. Consider what is being asked of you. Is a character required, and, if so, what kind? Is there a built-in conflict or must it be supplied? Can you predetermine a plot twist or a hook that will make your version of the scene unique?

In scenes that involve one dominant character and one straight character, you may take turns in a round-robin order. The first performer plays straight for the second performer, then the second performer plays straight for the third performer and so on. Eventually, the last performer plays straight for the first performer.

For whatever reason—fear, lack of inspiration, stalling—some people always prefer to be the last to get up to do an exercise. There are definite drawbacks to going last. Someone may have already used your idea. You may have thought about your idea so much that it will no longer feel spontaneous. Everyone may be bored by then.

Of course, there are drawbacks to going first as well. You can become the example of either what to do or what not to do. If possible, begin with people who have done the particular exercise before, or let the first group of performers repeat the exercise again at the end so that they, too, have a chance to see what kinds of things do or do not work.

You may find yourself repeating certain exercises because they are more beneficial or more challenging or just more fun. Having fun is an important part of performing comedy. For the audience to have a good time, the performers must be enjoying what they're doing.

GLOSSARY OF WORKSHOP TERMS

The following terms are used in the exercise and scene-setup descriptions. Here are their definitions for this text:

Performer: An improviser, an actor—this general term also includes callers and conductors.

Character: A persona that is assumed by the performer when playing a scene.

Dominant character: A character who becomes the focus for much of the humor in a scene. A scene or exercise may have more than one dominant character.

Straight character: A character whose job is to set up, draw out, and interact with the dominant character or characters in a scene. When playing straight, the performer assumes a role in the scene but doesn't usually adapt an extreme character trait, such as an accent or a character voice.

Caller: Required for certain exercises, the caller is a performer who remains off stage and calls out certain information to the performers on stage, in essence directing the exercise.

Conductor: Required for certain exercises, he conducts the performers, determining whose turn it is to speak by alternately pointing to one or more of them and cueing them in or out.

Exercise: An improv piece that has a structure to it and specific rules to play by. During the course of an exercise, the characters, the environment, and the plot may freely change.

Scene: An improv piece that maintains consistent characters, environment, and plot. It is based on a premise or scene suggestion.

Scene setup: A generic "scene suggestion" that is open-ended enough to be performed numerous ways, depending upon choices made by the performers. The workshop leader provides a basic setup—such as a location, a relationship, or an activity—and then each set of performers adds the other necessary elements when it is their turn to do the scene.

NOTE: The exercises and scene setups that follow are explained so that they may be used in a workshop situation. They are, however, the same set of exercises and scenes that you may include in a performance situation. Which ones you elect to use for that purpose are up to you. You will discover that some lend themselves more appropriately than others. In the workshop, the specific "suggestions" (locations, character traits, activities, types of relationships, etc.) required for each exercise or scene setup may come from either the workshop leader, fellow workshop members acting as an audience, or from the performers themselves participating at the time. When using these exercises or scene setups in a performance situation, the "suggestions" come exclusively from the audience. Also, note that, in a workshop situation, the "caller" or "conductor" is quite often the workshop leader, whereas these roles are played by members of the performing company during a show.

BEGINNING
AND GROUP WARM-UP
EXERCISES

"Yes, and . . ."

(Two or more performers)

This is the foundation of improvisation. It is a storytelling process for beginners. Any improv scene has a story to it, so you should get used to telling one. Here the story is told one line at a time. Select a group of two to six performers, depending upon the size of the workshop. They may line up across the front of the stage. The first actor makes a single, positive, declarative statement, such as, "It was a beautiful day at the park today." The next person continues the story with his own single, declarative statement, preceding it with "Yes, and . . ." For instance, "Yes, and many people came to enjoy it." Continue with the next person: "Yes, and it was difficult to find a place to picnic." Each new line should relate directly to the previous one, continually building the story. Not just a general statement about, in this instance, the park, but a statement that will further the particular story.

Be aware that you can add a "Yes, and . . ." but still introduce conflict. "Yes, and it was difficult to find a place to picnic" suggests an obstacle. The obstacle is the conflict. The conflict can lead you to the humor. "Yes, and we had to have our picnic by the fountain." "Yes, and at three o'clock when the fountain went off, we had soggy sandwiches and watered-down wine."

Continue until the story reaches a logical conclusion. For instance, "Yes, and at least the ants were washed away, so it wasn't a total loss."

[*Personal exercise*: Tell the entire story yourself, saying "Yes, and . . ." before each line.]

Laughing/Crying

(Two performers)

This exercise teaches actors to build a scene together. At the start, one will begin to laugh and the other will begin to cry. There is no predetermined story established between the actors. Each must devise his own particular backstory or reason for the emotional feeling he will play during the scene.

Without dialogue, the two actors establish a relationship and build the scene by reacting to each other emotionally. They should start off slowly and build in intensity. The more one cries, the more the other laughs and vice versa. If they work well together, it will become difficult to determine who is following the other.

Peaks and valleys are appropriate, as would happen naturally, and eye contact is important in order to "read" one another's actions. At a peak moment, the workshop leader can yell "switch," at which time the laugher begins to cry and the crier begins to laugh.

A variation of this exercise allows one actor to begin a dialogue at some point during the exercise, revealing his reason for laughing or crying. At this point, the other actor should let go of his own backstory, adjust to this now-established plot line, and together they build a scene.

Emotional Symphony
(Three to six performers and a conductor)

This is a presentational piece—performed directly facing the audience. Three to six performers form a small "orchestra" on the stage area, the conductor facing them with his back to the audience. Each performer chooses or is assigned an emotion, and, when pointed to by the conductor, verbalizes that emotion with vocal sounds but without the use any words. The conductor should orchestrate the piece by directing the performers' vocal entrances and exits and their intensity in "playing" their emotional instruments. He should build to a point at which two or more emotional instruments interact by playing simultaneously.

[*Personal exercise*: Practice verbalizing various emotions without the use of speech.]

Wandering Characters
(A group exercise with a leader)

The leader announces a particular kind of character, ranging anywhere from a naughty six-year old to a sentimental Hell's Angel to an angry librarian. The performers then simultaneously wander quietly about the stage area as if they are the designated character. After a while, the leader directs the performers to line the front of the stage and announces a particular subject about which, in character, the performers begin to speak. The performers should all speak at once and not concern themselves with what anyone else is saying. After the short monologues, repeat the process several times with various types of characters. This exercise enables everyone to experiment with trying on various new characters without the pressure of performing them alone on stage.

[*Personal exercise:* Create character's monologues by combining an occupation, an attitude, and topic of conversation.]

Story/Story

(Three to six performers and a conductor)

This is also a presentational piece, staged the same way as Emotional Symphony. A suggestion is taken for a first line for a story. It should be a single, declarative statement in third person, such as "Bill overslept, having forgotten to set his alarm clock." One performer begins telling a story starting with that line and continues until the conductor points to another performer, who is obligated to continue the story exactly where the previous performer left off. Try not to repeat the last word or phrase spoken by the previous actor before continuing. Try to keep the story grammatically correct. The conductor should try to switch speakers at key points in the story, such as when a new piece of information can be introduced. Varying the length of time allotted to each performer and switching storytellers in mid-sentence will make the exercise more interesting and challenging.

Three-Person Change of Emotion
(Three performers and a caller)

The three performers are given a location and a relationship. They begin a scene based on that information. As the action unfolds, the caller periodically announces various emotions, one at a time, to which all the performers simultaneously change. Although all are taking on this new emotion at the same time, each performer should find his own reason to change and have it affect his character differently. The caller should try to change emotions at key points in the scene to provide plot adjustments and twists.

[*Personal exercise:* Practice acting out different emotions.]

Person in the Middle
(Three performers)

Standing or sitting, three in a row, the two outside performers simultaneously tell stories to the person in the middle. The listener's job is to give equal focus to both storytellers and to retain as much of the two stories as possible. This is an exercise in listening as well as one in the art of storytelling. At the conclusion of the exercise, the person in the middle should try to summarize the two stories he was told.

[*Personal exercise:* Try simultaneously eavesdropping on two conversations.]

Hitchhiker with an Attitude

(Four to six performers)

Set up as many chairs, in the form of a car, as there are performers doing the exercise. Designate one person as the driver, who will pick up the others as hitchhikers. Each hitchhiker chooses an emotional attitude to play, and one at a time stands by the side of the road to be picked up. As each new rider enters the car, the people already inside take on this newest passenger's attitude. For example, the first hitchhiker may be "angry," and so the driver becomes angry as well until the next hitchhiker, who is "mysterious," is picked up, and then all three become mysterious. As each new passenger is picked up, give him the focus to establish his emotion before everyone joins in. This exercise is also good practice for pantomime as the actors should be aware of opening and closing of car doors, steering, and other parts of the automobile used.

Hitchhiker with an Accent

(Four to six performers)

This is the same as Hitchhiker with an Attitude except that accents or dialects are used instead of emotions. As each new hitchhiker enters the car, all the other passengers adopt his new accent.

[*Personal exercise*: Practice talking with different accents or dialects while you are driving in your car.]

Slap-Clap-Snap
(Three to twelve performers)

This may be done in a line facing the audience or in a circle if it involves the entire group at once. Together, everyone begins by rhythmically slapping their thighs, then clapping their hands, then snapping their fingers in unison (slap-clap-snap, slap-clap-snap, slap-clap-snap). Once this not-so-easy feat is in progress, one performer says a word. Then at the beginning of each sequence of slap-clap-snaps, the next person in line says a word that begins with last letter of the previous word. When the word association has gone around the entire circle and back to the first performer, the slap-clap-snap stops and that performer must begin a scene inspired by the word that he has just spoken. He may integrate other actors into the scene as necessary, and others may join the scene as they have ideas to further the action. The scene should be kept brief, and its conclusion can be marked by the group beginning the slap-clap-snap routine again. Continue word associating down the line or around the circle and stop again on the next person, who begins another scene. Continue until all have initiated a scene.

Use an Object in a Location

(One to six performers)

The first performer comes onto the stage and panto-
mimes an activity involving an imaginary object that is
inherent to a particular location. Either the group can
now guess the location and the activity, or another
performer who has determined the location can enter
the scene and pantomime another activity appropriate
to the same location. In a workshop situation, if the
workshop leader feels the second performer has misin-
terpreted the location, he should stop the action to
clarify. Continue with as many performers as you like,
each adding to the location by dealing with another
appropriate object and activity.

[*Personal exercise:* Practice pantomiming the use of
imaginary objects.]

Bus Stop

(One to three performers and a caller)

This is a silent exercise that can be done individually or in small groups. The performer chooses a reason to be waiting for a bus. If the exercise is done in groups, then the entire group agrees on a reason. They should pre-determine their individual ages, relationships to each other (if done in a group), and where they plan to go on the bus. Enter the scene, wait for the bus, and, when the caller announces that the bus has arrived, end the scene by boarding. The heart of the scene is what goes on while waiting at the bus stop. Without dialogue, the performers should be able to convey to the audience who they are, their relationship to each other, how old they are, and what their destination is. At the conclusion of the exercise, the audience can guess what information the performers were trying to convey.

The Argument

(At least six performers)

Begin with two performers, one on each side of the stage area. As they enter, they begin an argument, each having a strong point of view. Alternately, they are joined, one at a time, by performers who enter with a new self-righteous angle on the argument. As each new person enters, give him momentary focus to establish his point of view, then continue the group argument. Build until all have entered, then fade out the lights at the peak of the argument. This exercise is an energy builder as well as a lesson in "Yes, and . . ." in that it requires adding new information about a particular subject.

Freeze Tag
(Group exercise)

Known by several different names, this is a popular exercise that begins with two performers acting a scene inspired by a suggestion of a physical activity. They continue until some physical position assumed by one of them triggers an idea to a performer off stage, who yells "freeze." The performers on stage then freeze in that position. The new performer now enters the scene, "tags" and replaces one of the frozen performers, and assumes that performer's physical position. He then uses that physical position to initiate a change of action, relationship, and location to something completely different. The other actor in the scene adjusts to the new set of circumstances with his new partner, justifying the physical position in which he was frozen by verbally making it appropriate to the new situation. Continue the exercise until everyone has "tagged in" several times.

Freeze Tag (On the Word)
(Group exercise)

The same setup as regular Freeze Tag except that the action is frozen on a particular word or phrase rather than on a physical position. The new actor then uses that word or phrase to start a new scene.

Use an Object Before You Speak
(Two to four performers)

Play a scene with the added element of having to physically handle an imaginary object of some kind every time you speak. The object should be appropriate to the action of the scene. You may refer directly to the object you are handling or allow your manner in using the object to define what it is. This exercise is designed to make you aware of all the objects that are available to you in a particular environment and to get you used to doing activities during a scene.

The Harold
(A group exercise)

The Harold is a series of scenes that all pertain to a particular topic. Choose what the topic will be and take turns performing short scenes and monologues that are appropriate. Characters may recur during the course of the exercise to create running gags. The Harold should play as one continuous piece in that one scene should blend into another. The whole group should be on its feet and ready to jump in so, as one scene reaches a peak, another may begin. Scenes in The Harold don't generally run longer that a minute. The Harold can go on until the topic is exhausted. Pick a topic that is general enough to be dealt with in many ways, such as love, time, or money.

CHARACTER EXERCISES *

* (Note: A personal exercise appropriate to all of the
exercises in this section is to work to discover
and develop new characters whenever
you have free time.)

Dialect/Occupation/Emotion
(Two performers)

One performer chooses a dialect, an occupation, and an emotion, using all three to create a character. The other performer plays straight for this dominant character, acting as an appropriate foil. For instance, if the dominant character is a "flamboyant French decorator," the straight character might be a woman consulting with the decorator about furnishing her living room. Together, they build a scene.

Change of Ages
(Two to four performers and a caller)

Take a suggestion of a general location where there might be several people gathered, such as a doctor's waiting room or the rec room of a home. The performers begin the scene as children and then progressively age as the caller periodically announces new ages. The steps should be made in increments of about ten years. The exercise is more interesting if each performer remains the same character throughout his aging process. In this way, we can see how what happens to someone at an earlier age can influence him as he gets older.

Person on the Street

(Two performers)

One performer plays the interviewer while the other plays a person on the street. The setup is that the interview is being filmed, so it should be played as though a camera and boom (overhead) microphone are present. The interviewer, or host, is responsible for creating the kind of show and a reason for being out on the street talking to people. The character being interviewed should have a strong persona and respond to questions presented by the host of the show. Through the questioning process, you should learn not only facts about the character but also personality traits and opinions.

Teacher with an Accent

(Two performers)

One performer who is particularly adept at an accent should teach another how to do or make something appropriate to the culture of the place where the accent is used. For instance, with an Italian accent, teach someone to make pizza. With a Texan accent, teach someone to rope a steer. The performer playing the student will have the opportunity to learn the accent by repeating information as he learns it in the scene.

Animal Essence

(Two or three people)

Each person takes on the mannerisms of a different animal. This is not an exercise in imitation, but rather to adapt the essence of an animal to suggest a human character. Use posture, attitude, and ways of moving to become a character that suggests a type of animal, but don't actually act animal-like. For instance, if you choose to play a cat, don't lick yourself, or, as a dog, don't lift one leg to relieve yourself. Walking on "all fours" is not the idea here. As the "cat-type person," one might be forever grooming, move sensuously, perhaps even "curl up" to a friend. As a puppy, an abundance of energy is appropriate, as is being playful or even retrieving something discarded by another character. As far as dialogue is concerned, an appropriate vocal quality is suggested. Again, this does not include barking or meowing, but a subtle adjustment of the voice to suggest the animal, such as slow talking as a turtle or deep voiced and bellowing as a bear.

Place the actors in a neutral location together (e.g., a park, an airport terminal, a doctor's office) and let them get to know each other as they build a scene. Have the group guess the animals at the exercise's conclusion. This exercise is excellent for character development.

[*Personal exercise:* Practice developing characters based on the essences of various animals.]

Shades of a Character

(Two or three performers)

Choose a color and play a character who reflects it. Don't take the conventional literary choice. If the color is blue, don't be sad; if it's green, envious; or if it's yellow, frightened. Instead, try to play the essence of the color, whatever that means to you. The important thing is that you play something specific. At the conclusion of the exercise, guess the colors that have been portrayed.

Posing a Character

(One performer and a caller)

This sounds like a really silly exercise but it is actually very effective. The performer goes onto the stage area and strikes a series of poses using facial expressions and body postures. When one looks particularly interesting, the caller yells "freeze." The performer stops in that position and becomes the character he feels himself to be in that pose. The leader then asks questions of the character to find out more about him. Ask questions you would of any stranger you are getting to know, such as age, what they do for a living, where they're from. Based on the answers, move on to questions more specific to the character. This is a great way to create characters spontaneously.

Park Bench
(Two performers)

The setup is a park and a bench and anything else that goes along with it—trees, flowers, sunshine, picnics, dogs, children, birds, trash, Frisbees, and so on. Each character chooses a reason to be in the park. They can either pick a reason and then choose a character to go along with it or choose a character first and then pick a reason for being there. Allow the two characters to get to know each other as they play off each other to build a scene. Remember that your character should have had a life before he got to the park.

Waiting in Line
(Two to four performers)

Self-explanatory from its title, the exercise is just that—people waiting in line for anything: the bank, the post office, the DMV, or concert tickets. Choose a character who has a reason for being in that particular line. Relate to the other characters in the line and play the moments.

Waiting Room

(Two to four performers)

Not unlike Waiting in Line, these characters are also waiting. In this case they are in a room, waiting to see the doctor, the principal, the veterinarian, or maybe a potential employer. Each should have a reason for—and an attitude about—being there, and, of course, a life before coming into the scene.

Business Cards

(Two performers)

Get various types of business cards. One performer takes a card and creates a character and location based on the information provided on the card. The other performer plays straight by becoming a person who requires the service of that character. To make the exercise more challenging, both performers can take cards and create a scene based upon both occupations.

Bus Stop II (The Scene)

(Two to four performers)

A bus stop provides another location where characters can be explored while building a scene together. This expands upon the exercise Bus Stop by adding dialogue and a more extensive plot. The characters at the bus stop can either know each other or be strangers. They should each have a reason for being there and have had a life before arriving. A character may not necessarily be there to ride the bus at all. It might just be a place where that character hangs out. A character might be a wealthy executive whose car broke down and is forced to ride the bus for the first time. The options are endless.

Like Your Uncle Joe, for Instance

(One performer and a caller)

Choose someone from your life who has a memorable personality, maybe a teacher, a relative, or a roommate. Take the stage as a character based upon that person. The exercise is simply to maintain that character while answering questions posed by the audience. As in Posing a Character, the caller should ask questions as they would of any stranger they are getting to know, such as age, what the person does for a living, where he's from. The initial answers will lead the questioning to areas more specific to the character. Since your character is based on someone you know, you will already have a great deal of information about him and should be able to develop a well-defined character. Keep the character in your "bag of tricks" for use in any future situation that seems appropriate.

Talk Show
(Two performers)

One performer is the host of a TV talk show and is responsible for setting up the format of the show for the audience. It may range from a public-access show to one carried on an international satellite. The other performer is a guest on that show. The guest is responsible for whatever it is that makes him noteworthy—an accomplishment of some kind, be he an author, celebrity, sports figure, record breaker, etc. The host interviews the guest, working to draw out his character and trying to set him up with straight lines in the hope that he will have humorous responses.

Night School
(Four or five performers including a teacher)

Choose a subject that might be studied in night school. The exercise involves the characters of a teacher and three or four students. Make it the first night of class. This allows each character to take a moment to introduce himself and tell the rest of the class a little about himself, such as what he does for a living and why he is taking the class. The teacher can then begin the lesson. The students should behave and respond in a manner appropriate to their characters.

Panel

(Four performers including a moderator)

Choose a topic that's conducive to a panel discussion—perhaps a subject from the news or a controversial issue. Play the scene directly to the audience. One performer is designated as the moderator. He introduces himself and establishes the setting and tone of the discussion, be it a garden-club meeting at the town hall or a network television program like "Nightline." The panelists can then introduce themselves. They should be characters who have some connection with the topic. If possible, arrange for the characters on the panel to have differing opinions about it. As the moderator questions them, the characters will have a chance to develop as they express their views on the subject. Time permitting, open the questioning of the panel to the audience.

[*Personal exercise:* Read the newspaper or watch the news to be aware of what's going on in the world. The more information you have, the more prepared you will be for any improv situation. Be thinking of characters who are appropriate to various controversial issues and current events.]

Two Describe a Third
(Three performers)

A third performer waits off stage, listening to the first performer describe a character to the second performer that the third will have to become when he enters the scene. The description should include a physical, a vocal, and a personality trait, such as: "He uses his hands when he talks, he has an Italian accent, and he is passionate about everything he believes." The first performer also designates how the third character fits into the situation. For instance, number three might be a new coworker that number one has hired and number two will have to work with him. Once number three enters, number two should take the main responsibility for helping the new character by drawing out those traits during the rest of the scene. Stay away from cheap and perhaps less tasteful traits such as physical afflictions and bodily functions.

Three through the Door
(Two performers)

The setup is a huge store that sells anything you can think of. One performer plays the salesperson at the store. The other, over the course of three scenes, plays three different characters who enter the store one at a time to make a purchase. Make the three characters as different from each other as you can and select a purchase that is appropriate to each character. The salesperson should act as the straight character so that the main focus of each scene is on the customer. Each scene should only last about a minute. As soon as you leave as one character, come back in as another. A nice convention for this exercise, to save time and to keep it from becoming redundant, is for the customers to have exact change, a check, or, better yet, a running tab (trying to figure tax and make change seems to be counter-productive to the humor quotient). Don't, however, stifle any comedic urges you many have, like a character of a fur trapper coming into the store to buy Evian water and wanting to make his purchase on a barter system.

SCENE SETUPS *

* (Note: Whereas in the previous character exercises the goal was to get to know the characters themselves, these scene setups are designed to get the performers to consider how their characters will deal with a conflict. Each setup has a built-in general conflict. The choice of characters and specifics of the scene premise will determine the specifics of the conflict. The workshop leader may determine a specific premise for each group of performers, or he may leave it up to the performers themselves to decide. In either case, some piece of information must be established prior to the scene. For instance, for the first setup, Answering an Ad, what is being advertised should be determined before the scene starts. This will enable the performers to choose appropriate characters.)

Answering an Ad

(Two performers)

One character has advertised a product, a service, or a personal matter. The other character is responding to the ad. The focus in this scene is on how the two parties will deal with the specific thing that has been advertised. Therein lies the conflict. The characters will be determined by the specifics of the premise. For instance, if someone has advertised for a nanny, then the characters are the prospective nanny and the person interviewing her. This still leaves a lot of options. Obvious choices would be a middle-aged woman as the nanny and a young mother as the employer holding the interview. But the father might be holding the interview, and the prospective nanny might be an attractive young woman. Or the interview could be held by the child who is need of the nanny. Or the Nanny could be a man, or person from a foreign country, or a robot, or the child's real mother. There are many possibilities, but they are all based on the specifics of the premise.

Job Interview
(Two performers)

This exercise is self-explanatory from its title—one performer interviews another for a job. The interviewer should play straight for the person seeking the job. In other words, the job seeker will be the dominant character. In finding out the pertinent information necessary to know whether to hire the applicant, the interviewer will force the other performer to specifically define his character. The conflict lies in whether or not the applicant is suited for the job.

Buyer/Seller
(Two performers)

This scene involves one character selling something that the other character is considering buying. The conflict comes from the negotiation. To whom is the transaction most important? What compromise is each person willing to take? Again, the characters are based upon a specific premise that includes what is being sold and how the characters are affected by it. A person coming to buy a sports car will probably be different than someone coming to buy a food processor.

The Nuisance
(Two performers)

This exercise is done with no dialogue. Two strangers are seated next to each other at a performance—such as a lecture, a concert, or a play. One of them becomes a nuisance by displaying an annoying habit or trait that is distracting the other and keeping him from enjoying the performance. Examples of things that might be annoying include: taping your foot, sucking your teeth with your tongue, clearing your throat, mumbling, or heavy breathing. The annoyance should start off as a very subtle and occasional occurrence, then build in intensity as the scene progresses. Timing is an extremely important element in this exercise, as is the ability of the two characters to work together to build the scene. The nuisance should be aware of when the other character thinks he has finally stopped indulging his annoying habit, for that is the time to begin again.

Innocent Bystander

(Three performers)

The setup is that two people disagree about something and a neutral third party intervenes. The scene may take place anywhere: a home, a store, on the bus. Let the two arguers get started first and then have the innocent bystander either voluntarily offer an opinion or be dragged into the fray. In this case the characters and the conflict will be dependent upon each other and will probably be chosen simultaneously.

Three of a Kind

(Three performers)

Three performers play variations on the same type of character. At an appropriate location, there might be three clowns, three old people, three prisoners, or possibly three expectant fathers. Though they are the same type of character, they should all have different attitudes, depending upon their personal points of view. Three clowns, for instance, might have entirely different personalities from one another. One may be a retired acrobat who hates being a clown. Another may think that being a clown is the greatest thing on earth. Another might enjoy being a clown but is not very good at it. For a more intimate scene, do this structure with two characters. (If you do it with two characters, call it Two of a Kind.)

Coming Back From

(Three or four performers)

The premise is that everyone in the scene has just returned from one specific event, such as seeing a film, camping, attending a self-improvement seminar, or attending a recital. They are now gathered together to discuss the event. They each should have been influenced by what took place and have a very definite opinion about it. Their varying reactions to the event provide the conflict of the scene. Their attitudes will be directly related to their character. Who they are will determine how they feel. The location may be someone's home, a restaurant, or maybe a bar.

Authority Figure

(Two performers)

Each performer decides on a problem that would necessitate going to an authority figure of some kind. Take turns playing the authority figure and the person with the problem. Just prior to the scene, the performer with the problem can tell the other performer what kind of authority figure he should play. The scene is about the two of them trying to deal with the problem together.

Opposites React
(Two performers)

The setup is that two opposite types of characters clash as they cross paths. For instance, a yuppie leaving a fine restaurant is asked for money by a homeless person, a cynic meets a wide-eyed optimist at a party, or an elderly grandfather and his young grandson play a video game. These relationships can be set up prior to the scenes.

Reason for Being Late
(Two performers)

One character is waiting for the other character, who finally arrives late but has a reason for his tardiness. While the tardy character makes his excuse, the inconvenienced one establishes just what they are late for. The reason may be outrageous, but it must be played as though it really happened.

The Morning After
(Two performers)

It is the morning after an experience shared by two characters. They now must deal with the results in the light of day. How the characters behave this morning should be influenced by the events of the night before. As they struggle to deal with each other in this awkward situation, they can recall for each other and the audience their memory of the previous night. Examples of premises for this scene: a couple the morning after their honeymoon, two students who have pulled an all-nighter studying for an exam, or roommates facing their apartment after throwing a party the night before.

Three at Work
(Three performers)

The setup involves three people at their workplace dealing with the problems of the day as well as with each other. You may start with one person and have the other two make entrances. The conflict will arise out of the relationships between the people, some work-related event, or a combination of the two. Some character choices that have troublemaking potential: a mean boss, a new employee, the boss's daughter, a spy from another company, or an employee who went out with a fellow worker's boyfriend.

Ask a Favor

(Two performers)

Each performer thinks of a favor he would ask of someone. Take turns playing each role—the one asking and the one being asked. The asker should tell the other performer what their relationship is going to be— such as best friend, boss, or father—so that he may play an appropriate character and set up the appropriate environment on stage. The asker can then enter and ask the favor. The nature of the favor should be arrived at fairly early into the scene, but not before defining the characters and their relationship to each other for the audience. The askee should resist being accommodating in order to build a conflict and should make the asker work for his goal. The favor itself can be anything, but obviously it should not be something too easy to fulfill. The reason for the favor is often where the humor comes from. For instance, asking to borrow money is not particularly funny, but the reason for needing the money may be. Don't put any restrictions on yourself. You can be anything from a teenager asking his dad to borrow the car to an angel new to Heaven asking to borrow a veteran angel's wings for the night.

Patent Office

(Two performers)

Each person thinks of an original invention that has not yet been produced. Take turns playing a patent officer and a person coming into the office to patent an invention. The inventor should truly believe that his invention is going to change the world. To build the conflict and to provoke the inventor into really trying to sell his invention, the patent officer should show resistance. The invention itself need not be something that could actually exist, but it should be dealt with as if it could. In other words, play the scene legitimately.

Reason to Get Drunk

(Two performers)

Each performer thinks of a reason to get drunk. It can either be a happy or a sad occasion. Take turns playing the bartender and the drinker. The bartender's job is to help the drunk tell his story by lending an ear and asking appropriate questions. You can build the suspense of the scene by giving some background information before coming right out with your reason for drinking.

Door-to-Door Salesperson
(Two performers)

One performer chooses a product to sell door-to-door. The other performer plays the person at home. Take turns playing both roles. Don't limit yourself to items that are traditionally sold door-to-door. Think of items that you might not expect a person to sell in this fashion, like used cars. To build conflict in the scene, the resident should not be eager to buy.

Important Phone Call
(Two performers)

Each performer thinks of an urgent phone call to make. Take turns playing the caller and the recipient of the call. Prior to the scene, the caller should tell the recipient who he will be playing so that he may answer the phone appropriately. Don't be limited in whom you call. You can be a teenager calling a girl for the first time to make a date. You can be Noah calling God to ask him if you should include spiders as part of your collection of animals.

Visitor from the Past
(Two performers)

The scene is between two people who have not seen each other for a long time. Each performer thinks of someone who might have been in their past, such as a teacher, a first love, or the school bully. Create a reason to see this person again. Tell them who they are and begin the scene. Alternate playing each role.

First Session
(Two performers)

One of the performers plays a character who provides a service. The other plays a character who has need for that service. Since it is the first encounter, there is an opportunity to get to know the characters and to explore the problem of the person seeking the service. Examples of appropriate services: hairdresser, therapist, chiropractor. Take turns playing each role.

Last Session
(Two performers)

This exercise can be done independently or in tandem with First Session (see above). When done together, the two scenes should be done back to back, and the chosen service should be one that requires subsequent visits. They should also tie together—the last-session scene should make reference to and be influenced by the first session. The performers can also address the reason for it being the last session.

Premise Scenes
(As many performers as are required)

These are simply scenes based on premises. There are no restrictions. Either make up an idea or take a suggestion of something like "being pulled over by a policeman," "having the boss over for dinner," or maybe "moving to a new city." Either choose the premise and then pick the performers to play it out or choose the performers first and then create a premise to suit them. This is the purest and most challenging of all improv structures.

ADVANCED EXERCISES

Change of Emotions
(Two performers and two callers)

This is my personal favorite improv exercise. It seems to work best when involving two strangers who share a common experience, such as doing laundry, having a drink at a bar, or enjoying a day in the park.

Two callers, one for each onstage performer, first get a list of emotions or states of mind from the audience (e.g., fear, confusion, elation, paranoia, naiveté) and a location in which to begin the scene. Once the location has been established and a relationship is struck up between the two characters, the callers begin to control the characters and their relationship by calling out from the list of emotions, thus changing the onstage characters' emotions one at a time. The caller's function is to set up his respective performer with an appropriate emotional change that will further the plot of the scene.

Listening is of utmost importance in this exercise, both on the part of the onstage performers and the callers. The humor in this exercise comes from the adeptness of the performer to change his emotion while still maintaining the flow of the scene. Callers should take turns initiating their changes in order to give time to each performer to establish his new emotion. Be aware that it is not necessary to speak immediately upon changing emotion. An emotion can be portrayed just as effectively though physical behavior until it is appropriate to speak.

Playbook

(Two performers)

This exercise requires a book of scenes from plays, such as *Great Scenes From The World Theater.* One performer reads a character's dialogue from a scene of a play. The other performer improvises dialogue to go with it, thus creating a whole new scene. An occupation is chosen for the improviser to give him a character to play. While the performer with the text starts on stage, the improvising actor makes an entrance and says the first line. For instance, if the occupation is doctor, the first line might be "I have the results of your X-rays." The reader then reads the first line of dialogue from a character in the play. Then the job of the improviser is to justify that line to the scene, even though it probably has nothing to do with X-rays, by responding in the character of the doctor. The improviser should never ask questions of the reader because an answer will very likely not be in the written script. The two performers continue to exchange dialogue as the improviser continues to justify whatever line is thrown at him. If a long speech comes up in the script, the actor reading may use just the first sentence of the speech. This is an important exercise in listening and for being flexible in a scene.

First Line/Last Line
(Two performers)

Before the scene begins, choose two lines of dialogue. One will be the first line of the scene, the other will be the last. The lines should not apparently relate to each other. The performer who says the first line should later take responsibility for helping the other performer get to the last line. This is an exercise in building a scene together, learning to recognize where another improviser is going and helping him to get there.

One-Minute Blackouts
(Two performers and a caller)

This exercise consists of a series of mini-scenes. Each scene begins in the dark with two performers having no preconceived notion of who or where they are. The caller announces a location—such as a furniture store, a playground, or a health club—and the lights come up on the stage. As quickly as possible, the two performers must establish who they are and what is going on between them. End the scene by dimming the lights within one minute, whether it is completed or not. Each set of two performers can do three scenes in a row.

Hidden Agenda

(Two performers)

Choose a simple premise, such as a business meeting or a social engagement of some kind. One of the characters should then be assigned a hidden agenda—that is, it is his goal to get the other person to do something. The goal should be accomplished with as much subtlety as possible so that the rest of the group will have difficulty guessing what the hidden agenda was at the end of the scene. It need not be anything very complicated. It is also not necessary for the goal to be accomplished for the scene to be a success. Just the fact that you are trying to get the other person to do something without coming out and saying it will give you a different perspective on how you behave in the scene. Some possible examples of hidden agendas: get the person to open a window, get the person to offer you their seat, get the person to offer you money.

Poet/Translator
(Two performers)

This piece is played directly to the audience. One performer recites an original poem, one line at a time, in gibberish but as if he is speaking the language of a specific foreign country. The other performer, sharing the stage with the poet, translates each line for the audience. The translator may also speak with the appropriate accent of the country if desired. As they alternate speaking, the translation should echo the dramatic interpretation of the poet, and the poet should resume the story of his poem from where the translator leaves off. This exercise benefits from listening and working to build the poem together.

Before beginning, get a suggestion of a first line for an original poem. If you are adept at accents, you may also ask for a suggestion of a foreign country. If not, choose an accent that you are familiar with. The translator may choose a venue for the recitation of the poem and begin the performance by introducing himself and the poet.

Subtitles

(Four performers)

This is similar to the Poet/Translator but involves four performers. Two of them play characters in a foreign-language film (speaking gibberish). The other two, standing off stage, provide verbal subtitles that translate the film into English for the audience. Listening is of utmost importance in this exercise, to help build a story and to keep from talking over each other. Remember to let each gibberish line be translated before the next line is spoken.

Dubbing

(Four performers)

This exercise has the same setup as Subtitles, except this time the onstage characters merely move their lips as they pretend to speak. The offstage performers supply the voices, working to sync the dialogue to their counterpart's mouths. The onstage performers may lead the dubbers by supplying physical activity and facial expression, prompting appropriate or appropriately inappropriate dialogue.

Foreign Restaurant

(Three or four performers)

This is a scene designed to allow the performers to practice accents and to use words and dialogue appropriate to that accent. It takes place in a restaurant that serves some type of ethnic cuisine. The customers can be Americans, but the staff of the restaurant are all of a chosen ethnic origin. Staff members may be waitpersons, cooks, or maitre d's. If the performers are proficient at doing dialects, let the audience choose the type of restaurant. This scene allows for practice in playing characters, and using entrances and exits, as well as in using dialects.

Split Screen
(Four performers)

The stage is divided into two areas so that two scenes may take place at the same time. The two scenes should relate to one another and should alternate in taking focus. An example of this format might be set at a high-school prom. The stage area would be divided into a boys' bathroom on one side and a girls' bathroom on the other. In the boys' room, two guys would be talking about their dates while the girls would be in the other room talking about the boys. Although the performers and the audience actually hear what is being said in both rooms, the characters do not. The humor comes from using the information that you supposedly don't hear to influence what you say. You are able to comment on what is being said in the other scene without actually acknowledging that you heard it.

Style Spot

(Two to five performers and caller)

It certainly helps if you're familiar with legitimate theater, playwrights and their works, and theatrical styles to do this exercise. The workshop leader or an audience member suggests a small, mundane problem a family might have, such as whose turn it is to take out the garbage. Begin the scene and continue until the caller freezes the action to announce a style of theater or the name of a playwright, such as melodrama, Kabuki, Commedia dell'arte, Arthur Miller, Ionesco, or Shakespeare. Continue the scene in that style or as that particular playwright would have written it. When continuing the action in the playwright's style, try to resist using actual dialogue from one of his plays or even incorporating one of his plots. Rather, try to capture the flavor and style of his writing and adapt it to the plot being developed in your scene. You may either compile a list of theater styles and playwrights prior to the scene or turn to the audience each time you call freeze and ask them to provide a suggestion. The entire exercise may be played by the same group of performers or some may make entrances and exits as appropriate to the plot.

Who Am I?

(Group exercise)

Someone leaves the room (out of earshot), and, upon his return, must guess what famous person the others have decided that he has become. The exercise is done in the form of a scene, but the improviser who has left the room doesn't know what character he is playing. The clues come in how the others now refer to him in the scene. They, of course, cannot say his name or make any direct reference to who he is. As the guesser begins to think he knows who he is, he should begin to adopt that person's persona and say things that person would say. If it becomes apparent that he is wrong, he should lay back and listen some more until he has another idea of who he might be. Always continue in the form of a scene. Resist asking questions like "Did I chop down a cherry tree?" or "Am I George Washington?" Begin with one or two performers and the guesser. Others may enter the scene as they have ideas for clues but should exit once they have served their purpose so as not to have too many people on stage at once. This exercise is a good one for character development.

Phrase Am I

(Group exercise)

I know the name makes no sense, but that's what I've heard it called for years. A variation of the exercise Who Am I?, Phrase Am I challenges the performer to guess and use a common phrase or aphorism, like "The grass is always greener on the other side of the street," that the others have chosen while he has left the room. Played in the form of a scene, the premise should reflect the meaning of the phrase. For instance, if the phrase is "the grass is always greener . . .", the scene should be about jealousy. The clues should come through the theme of the scene so as to lead the guessing performer to naturally say the phrase in the context of what's going on around him. Start the scene with one other performer besides the guesser, then others may enter and exit and give subsequent clues. The scene ends when the guesser uses the phrase as part of his dialogue.

Hidden Line

(Two performers)

Each performer in the workshop writes a simple line of dialogue onto a separate piece of paper and throws them into a hat. Before beginning the scene, one of the performers picks a line from the hat, and he must incorporate that line into the scene. He should build the plot of the scene so that the line of dialogue fits seamlessly into the story. It should, in fact, be difficult for the audience to guess what was the given line at the conclusion of the scene. Even though the other performer doesn't know the hidden line of dialogue, he should help his fellow performer by working with him to build the story in whatever direction he is leading it. To make this exercise more challenging, have both performers pick a piece of paper and work together to help one another discreetly drop in their lines.

Scene to Song Title

(Two to four performers)

Break up into groups of two to four performers. Each group chooses a well-known song and creates a scene reflecting the meaning of its title. Resist using the title literally. Use it as a theme for the scene. For instance, if the title is "I Left My Heart In San Francisco," the scene might be about someone enduring a long-distance relationship rather than being about an organ donor. The rest of the groups can guess each title at the scene's conclusion.

Alter Ego

(Four performers)

Similar in setup to Subtitles, two performers are on stage while two others remain off stage. The onstage characters create a scene together, but, after each line of dialogue, the coinciding offstage voice says what the character is really thinking. Give and take is an integral element here, as is listening. The same technique used in the exercise Split Screen is useful here. The onstage performers, privy to what their alter egos are saying, can use the information to influence how their characters behave and react to one another.

One Word at a Time

(Two performers) ˙

This exercise shows how much information can be conveyed with only one word, perhaps accompanied by an attitude, a gesture, or a facial expression. In this two-character scene, only one word may be spoken at a time. Once a character has spoken a word, he may not speak again until the other character has spoken. The scene continues, one word at a time. It is an exercise in economy of dialogue. A common mistake of improvisers is that they tend to over-talk a scene, saying much more than is necessary. This is also a lesson in using more activities in a scene rather than relying on dialogue to carry it. The scene can be based on a simple premise provided by the workshop leader or by the audience.

One Sentence at a Time
(Two performers)

This scene has the same rules and setup as One Word at a Time except that, in this case, the performers may use only one sentence at a time. To not defeat the purpose of the exercise, alternate speaking so that the performers cannot run two sentences together.

No Questions
(Two performers)

This is a two-person scene with the restriction that no questions may be asked. The purpose is to get the performers used to adding information, to furthering the scene, and to making assumptions, rather than laying the burden on the other performer to further the action by asking him questions. Review the exercises "Yes, and . . ." and Story/Story as they are similar in their story-building techniques. The scene can be based on a simple premise provided by the workshop leader or the audience.

Transformation
(Two performers)

This is a difficult exercise to do as well as to explain. It is somewhat like if you did six Freeze Tags in a row with the same two performers without stopping to freeze the action. Choose beginning and ending occupations for both performers. They begin the scene, each playing their opening occupation. Then, as the scene progresses, they will transform themselves through a series of different roles or occupations until the scene finally ends when the performers reach their ending occupations. The transitions may be signaled with either physical or vocal change. For instance, one performer may be a pizza-delivery person holding out a large pizza with both hands. He may then transform that physical position by becoming a doctor, holding his hands out as if they have just been scrubbed clean. In this case, the other performer can immediately become his nurse and begin to fit his hands with rubber gloves.

This is an exercise in following another performer. When one performer makes a transition to a new character or occupation, the other performer follows by becoming an appropriate counterpart. There is not a continuous plot. Either performer may change character or occupation at any given time, so both must be flexible and ready to follow. Go through a total of five or six changes during the exercise.

Slow-Start Scene

(Two performers)

Two performers come onto the stage area with no pre-conceived ideas—no premises nor characters, minds a blank. Then, in no hurry, they allow a scene to evolve. If minutes go by without any dialogue, it's okay. Eventually one of the performers will feel as though he is somewhere for some reason and begin to relate this information to the other performer. The other performer should then adapt accordingly, and together they build the scene. This exercise encourages performers to feel free to enter a scene completely open-mindedly to see what happens once they get there. It also helps them to be able to adjust to whatever information evolves.

Rashomon

(Three performers)

In this exercise, the same basic scene is repeated three times in a row, once from each character's point of view. In each variation, one of the characters is the dominant figure while the others play supporting roles in the scene. Based on Kurosawa's *Rashomon*, it investigates how different characters perceive the same event.

Option Play
(Two performers and a caller)

A suggestion is taken of a relationship between two performers. Once a relationship and a location have been established, the caller periodically "freezes" the action to ask the audience specific questions about what they would like to see happen next. The performers then integrate each new idea into furthering the action of the scene. For instance, if the relationship is that of teacher and student and the scene is developing in the classroom after regular school hours, the caller might ask, "Why has the teacher kept the student after school?" or, "This student has a secret; what is it?" Continue until the scene has played itself out.

Pitching an Idea
(Three or four performers)

This is an exercise in building an idea together. The cast of the scene is a creative team of some kind, such as a group of ad executives, auto designers, or film producers. They are given a kind of product to create and are to build a marketing campaign around it. There should be no denial, as each performer adds to the others' ideas. This exercise should incorporate the principle of the exercise "Yes, and . . ."

Make a Song
(One or more performers and a musician)

Improvise a song, based on a style of music and an original title or first line provided by the audience or the workshop leader. The singer and musician should work together, following each other to create a melody and structure for the song. This exercise requires a lot of practice to gain proficiency.

Audition
(Four or five performers, including a director)

Choose a theatrical situation that requires an audition. It might be for a musical or a play. It might be for a local theater company, for a Broadway production, or even for a prison holiday-show. One performer is designated the director and is responsible for setting up the environment for the audience. Each auditioner then introduces himself, gives his credentials, and presents some type of audition for the role to which he is suited. Auditioners may perform a monologue, sing a song, dance, or play the spoons—whatever displays their talent. Whether the character actually is talented or not, he should always try his best when auditioning.

Bookbeat

(Three or four performers and a conductor)

This exercise uses the same technique as Story/Story. In this case, each performer chooses a well-known author and, when pointed to by the conductor, continues the story in the style of that author. Remember not to repeat or overlap the dialogue of the previous speaker. The audience or workshop leader can suggest an original first line to get started. To make it more challenging, allow the audience to suggest the authors used.